REMEMBERING

HAVERHILL

REMEMBERING

HAVERHILL

stories from

THE MERRIMACK VALLEY

CHARLES W. TURNER

Charleston   London

THE
History
PRESS

Published by The History Press
Charleston, SC 29403
www.historypress.net

All images were taken from the Haverhill Public Library, Special Collections, and used with their permission.

First published 2008

Manufactured in the United States

ISBN 978.1.59629.553.7

Library of Congress Cataloging-in-Publication Data

Turner, Charles W.
Remembering Haverhill : stories from the Merrimack Valley / Charles W. Turner.
p. cm.
ISBN 978-1-59629-553-7
1. Haverhill (Mass.)--History--Anecdotes. 2. Haverhill (Mass.)--Social life and customs--Anecdotes. 3. Merrimack River Valley (N.H. and Mass.)--History--Anecdotes. 4. Merrimack River Valley (N.H. and Mass.)--Social life and customs--Anecdotes. 5. Turner, Charles W.--Childhood and youth--Anecdotes. 6. Haverhill (Mass.)--Biography--Anecdotes. I. Title.
F74.H5T87 2008
974.4'5--dc22
2008027633

CONTENTS

Preface   7

The Little River   9
A Monumental Journey   13
Hannah's Lost Monument   19
A Frontier Settlement   23
Bridging Time   29
Catholicism Comes to Haverhill   35
Life in the Merrimack Valley   41
Old King Coal   45
The Railroad Comes to Haverhill   49
A City Burning   53
The Phoenix Rises   57
The Old Downtown Clock   61
The Birth of Saint James Grammar School   65
An Old-Fashioned Winter   71
An Ill Wind Blows   77
The Old Ways of Life   81
The Peddlers   87
Living a Pedestrian Life   91
The War Years   95
The Winds of Change   99
The Train Wreck   105
Boulevard of Dreams   109
Back Street Blues   115
A Troubled Bridge   119
Location, Location, Location   123

About the Author   127

Preface

The world in which we live has not been around for very long. It came to be the way it is after the most recent ice age, which took place around ten thousand years ago. The hills, valleys and the general terrain that we now see remained when the ice retreated. Man first came to live in this area as he followed animals along the edges of the ice, but our forefathers did not settle in North America until 1620.

Haverhill, Massachusetts, was founded in 1640. There were no roads, but there were rivers to travel on, and these waterways provided power for the mills needed to maintain a settlement. It was a new and strange land that was actually inhabited by others when our country's founders moved into this part of the world. This was a period known as colonization, with France to our north and Spain to the south and west.

At the outset, we were at the mercy of France and England, both of which fought their European wars in their western colonies. Settlers living in the early community of Haverhill were living where Indians and the French could attack them at any time. Many of the settlers died or were taken prisoner to New France. Some were ransomed, but others chose to stay with the French.

In this book, I have collected twenty-five short articles that will take you back to this beginning and through the few hundred years that our community has been around. Haverhill was a plantation at first, and the early settlers worked hard just to survive. Over the years, the plantation grew into a community that became known as the "Queen Slipper City," as most of the city's residents worked in shoe shops. This trade ultimately disappeared during my lifetime.

Haverhill residents enjoyed good times and experienced bad times as well. My tales will bring some of these events to you. As I wrote, I realized how yesterday's stories have had an impact on my life. I realized how a short life, such as my own, has witnessed so many things that no longer exist today. They are now part of our historical past and should be mentioned so that they will never be forgotten.

I started working on my family genealogy in 1990 and began doing research for Graig Laing (deceased) at the Haverhill Public Library, Special Collections. Gerry Molina (deceased), editor of the *Haverhill Gazette*, got me started as a writer in 1998, and I have published more than two hundred stories since then. Both of these men aided me as I learned about history, and with the assistance of others, I eventually wrote this book.

My son, Charles F. Turner, provided computer support, and my grandson, Joseph W. Gemmell, introduced me to Flaredrive. Drew Laughlan, of Haverhill Public Library, Special Collections, aided in scanning my images, and Kurt Seastrand, my brother-in-law, helped me with the manuscript transmission. I also thank my wife, Evie, who had to sit through fifty years of storytelling.

In the end, I leave my town to those who will live here in the future. Ours is an interesting story of a plantation that grew into a city and all of the problems associated with such growth. I hope that these articles will provide a history that can be enjoyed by those who read them.

THE LITTLE RIVER

The Little River flows through the center of Haverhill, drawing little or no notice from passersby. It isn't much as rivers go, especially when one considers the great rivers of the world, but it played a major role in the settlement and development of Haverhill in its early days.

Thousands of years ago, a retreating ice cap deposited a large number of low hills where we now live. They are known as drumlins and do not exceed four hundred feet in elevation. About twenty of these drumlins form a bowl-shaped piece of terrain that begins in Kingston, New Hampshire, and ends near the shores of the Merrimack River. The Little River flows south through this area, collecting waters from many small tributaries on its way to join the Great River, our Merrimack River.

A tribe of Pennacook Indians found the river pleasant enough to set up a village at a spot near where Winter Street now crosses over it. Only a few survivors of the tribe remained when English settlers appeared in 1640. In 1642, two of the tribe's leaders signed a deed that transferred ownership of their land, Pentucket, to the settlers. The sale price was three pounds, ten shillings.

The small river is of primary importance in the original deed, for it is used as the reference point that established Pentucket's boundaries. Measured from "ye little river," the limits were set at eight miles west, six miles east and six miles north—a rather substantial piece of real estate for the price.

In the beginning, the early settlers remained closer to the area near Mill Street, where they set up five mills on a stream that flowed south from Plug Pond to the Merrimack River. If you think that the Little River is somewhat obscure, I challenge you to find anything that remains of the Mill Street stream. The Little River was known as the West River during those early years.

In 1651, as the local population began to exceed the limited capability of the existing mills, permission was granted to build a sawmill on the West River. The village also needed the sawmill to provide material for the growth with which it was faced. The Little River then came to be known as the Saw Mill River.

In addition to the power it supplied, the waters of the Little River were alive with migrating fish as they worked their way to spawning grounds located farther upstream, even as far north as Great Pond, which is now called Kenoza Lake. "Wears" were set in the stream to capture alewife, in particular, along with salmon and shad. The villagers used some of this bounty for themselves and created a fishing industry that lasted into the 1800s.

A number of other mills were erected along the banks of the Saw Mill Rill River during the late 1600s and throughout the 1700s. There was a corn grinding mill, a gristmill and a fulling mill, all of which used the river as a source of power. In 1804, Ezekiel Hale Sr. built a cotton mill and began a textile industry. This industry was the forerunner of a manufacturing tradition that raised Haverhill to international status.

Hale saw the river as an important, if not vital, element to the growth of his business and the prosperity of the town. He built a scrabble dam as a means of controlling the river's flow and improving its reliability as a

The Little River provided power for the Stephen's Mill, located on Winter Street in Haverhill. Young boys are shown playing on its ice-covered surface.

power source. By 1832, Hale had a sawmill, grain mill and a flannel factory operating at the dam.

In 1835, a major fire destroyed Hale's flannel mill, which he had constructed from wood. He replaced it with a red brick structure that continues to stand beside the waterfall on Winter Street. If you look closely at its south side, the overshot wheel raceway is still visible.

Hale spent much of his life working to ensure a constant source of water for his mills. He also spent considerable amounts of money improving the backwaters of Hale's River, as it came to be known. He even petitioned the village to permit the installation of a flume at Great Pond to regulate its release of waters during dry periods. During 1855, Hale held an auction and sold his business to Captain Nathaniel Stevens, a textile manufacturer located in Andover's North Parish. The Stevens family continued to own and operate the mill well into the 1900s.

The advent of steam and electric power resulted in a diminishing interest in Little River. No longer was it needed to run the small cluster of mills at the waterfall. It became a conveyer of sewage and animal waste from a slaughterhouse located upstream, in Rosemont. Because the Little River is a tidal stream up to the waterfall, this presented a problem as effluents backed up in the river twice a day during high tide.

Material lodged in the nooks and crannies along the river's bottom and was very objectionable at times. Studies were conducted about how to cure the problem, and attempts even included using high-powered hoses to wash the odor away at low tides. The Little River was finally enclosed in a concrete tunnel that carried it beneath Washington Square to where it discharged into the Merrimack River.

Through the years, some residents used the Little River for recreational purposes. Some fished its waters, which were home to released trout, hornpout, pickerel, perch and other species. Others bathed in the river or found relief from the heat of summer in its cool depths. Many enjoyed ice-skating on its frozen surfaces during the winter months. These activities continued up to recent times, and many who are living today can still recall the good times they enjoyed on the Little River.

The Little River was not only important to the growth of Haverhill, but it also had an impact on many lives by virtue of its existence. Because the river was a reliable source of power that resulted in the establishment of manufacturing facilities, many workers moved to Haverhill to find employment there. Such was the case for my English ancestor, Charles Turner, who was born in West Yorkshire in 1828.

In their North Andover mill, the Stevens family employed Turner in the manufacturing of textiles. He came to Haverhill in 1863 to work in the mill's

CORPS OF ENGINEERS, U.S.A.
Haverhill, Mass.   Flood Control
Boston District   Force Account
Looking downstream from Locke
Street bridge on Little River.
201-1523.3   Sept. 22, 1937

The Little River is tidal and returned debris to the falls twice a day. A high-pressure hose was unsuccessfully used to try to cleanse its bottom.

carding room. His first wife had died while giving birth to their fifth child, and he remarried a widow. His second wife was a neighbor in Andover and had three children of her own.

At the Steven's Mill, Turner replaced his brother-in-law, who left the company to start his own business. Turner bought his home in Haverhill and moved to the end of Harrison Street, which was close to the mill and was near the only Catholic church in Haverhill. His oldest son met and married an Irish girl, Maria Fennelly, an event that resulted in my family becoming Catholic and living in the Acre. Charles Turner remained a Protestant and was rather bigoted toward this Irish girl. In a way, this sums it up. If it hadn't been for the Little River, I wouldn't be here today. If you find fault with this, blame it all on the river. Bigotry doesn't count in this case.

A Monumental Journey

Hannah Duston was the first woman in this country to have a statue erected in her honor. However, while Haverhill may claim her as its own, other towns boast similar dedications to her memory.

Much has been recorded about Hannah's exploits, but many details are missing about the events that surround her captivity. She was taken by a band of marauding Indians during a raid in 1697 and managed to escape under grisly circumstances. Haverhill residents are surrounded by constant reminders of this pioneer woman in the form of monuments located throughout the city. I recently decided to visit them—a monumental undertaking—and this is what I found.

Haverhill, Massachusetts

At GAR Park, I examined the beautiful statue of Hannah that was erected there in 1879. It is the work of sculptor C.H. Weeks and is a bronze, life-size image of a woman in modest attire who is obviously angry. The statue stands fifteen feet tall and has a green patina that attests to its antiquity. Four bronze plaques attached to its granite pedestal tell the tale that history has recorded.

Hannah appears as the major performer in the scenes depicted on the plaques. A boy captive, Samuel Leonardson, is portrayed as a small child, but he was fourteen years old at the time and very much a young man. A tablet shows Hannah paddling a canoe from a bow position with Samuel curled up in the stern. Samuel was actually old enough to have been of great assistance in handling a canoe on the swift, swollen spring waters of the Merrimack River.

My next stop was at a large millstone marker on River Street, near Bradley's Brook, where Hannah beached the canoe on her return from captivity. I looked out at the silt-laden waters that swept past the spot and

A commemorative monument marks the landing spot of the first settlers in Pentucket. They came by boat up the Merrimack River in 1640.

didn't envy her time on the Merrimack River. It was no doubt worse in 1697 because there were no flood-control facilities on the river at that time.

I visited the huge stone monument set on a very small plot on Monument Street that is purported to be the spot where Hannah died while living out her final years with a son. The name Martha appears with Hannah's name on the stone, and this refers to the infant daughter who was killed by the Indians during the 1697 raid. The monument is located opposite Haverhill High School, not very far from the stone garrison house built by Hannah's husband on Hilldale Avenue.

BOSCAWEN, NEW HAMPSHIRE

I was particularly interested in a monument that marked the site where Hannah had spent her last night in captivity. It was a campsite located on a small island, where the Contoocook River flows into the Merrimack River six miles north of Concord.

Hannah escaped during the late hours of March 30, 1697, and I had timed my visit to coincide with that date. The sky was gray and it was early spring cold as I walked along a path leading to the island. Rusting rails of the old Northern Railroad had once crossed the island, using it as a stepping-stone across the mouth of the Contoocook River.

I crossed over the river and continued to follow the rails to a small clearing, where I found myself looking at an enormous gray granite monument located in the middle of nowhere! It stood twenty-five feet high with a statue of a large woman atop a pedestal. Her back was to the river, which puzzled me until I realized that she was positioned that way for the benefit of train passengers going by.

The monument was erected in 1874 and is made from Concord granite. Inscriptions on it shed very little light on the event that took place there. An original donor wrote in 1902 that he "hoped that the state may at some time cover [the monument] with bronze tablets" that indicate the main points of this tragic story. This has yet to happen.

The statue is of a woman dressed in less than her best, holding a hatchet and fresh scalps in her hands. Looking at her, I felt that I wouldn't want to mess with her, especially since she appeared to have an axe to grind. Her nose had been shot off, and the monument was covered with painted graffiti. I walked about the small island and found it to be very gray, muddy and not very pretty early in the spring. With water flowing around it on all sides, it would have been a campsite isolated from those in pursuit.

Hannah Duston was captured by Indians in 1697 and taken to Boscawen, New Hampshire, on the Merrimack River. A monument was raised in her memory there.

NASHUA, NEW HAMPSHIRE

My journey took several days as I searched out the various monuments associated with Hannah's life. Once leaving the island, she was afraid that she might be followed, even though she had destroyed the canoes she left behind. As the day became brighter, she looked for a place to hide, and young Samuel must have told her about a place he knew in Dunstable, an area we now know as Nashua.

16

The trio pulled into a small stream and continued to paddle a few hundred yards to where John Lovewell lived. He was one of the earliest settlers in this area. I found the site marked by a very small gravestone-type monument located at the intersection of Allds and Fifield Streets. There is nothing to see here, but it is interesting to note that the spot is located about a quarter mile from the Merrimack River.

Barre, Massachusetts

During May 1967, a man named John Dustin appeared in Barre looking for a statue of his famous ancestor. Nobody could help him, but an appeal appeared in the local newspaper that set research wheels in motion. The Barre Historical Society found documentation showing that their Civil War monument was originally dedicated to Hannah Duston back in Haverhill!

On June 7, 1861, the Duston Monument Association erected a twenty-five-foot-tall Italian marble obelisk at the site of the original attack in Haverhill. A great amount of inscription appeared on it, especially concerning the genealogical association of Hannah's children. The obelisk was to be paid for mostly by subscriptions.

The family had a disagreement about the spelling of the name (Dustin versus Duston) and whether the monument was being erected in the proper place. Disenchanted, people withdrew their pledges, and the bill went unpaid until the end of the Civil War. The marble shaft was sold at an auction to a man from Woburn, who removed the inscriptions and family details from it.

At the conclusion of the war, Barre, a small rural community, was looking for a monument to honor fifty-nine young men who never returned from the conflict. The town eventually purchased the "used" column, and it now stands, quite beautifully, on a common in the center of the town. Just follow Route 62 as far west as it goes and you can see it for yourselves.

My search revealed that New Hampshire adopted Hannah and can claim that it was the first state to erect a statue in her memory. The children in Boscawen's fourth grade write an annual report on her each year, but the Town of Barre owns the first monument actually dedicated to the memory of Hannah Duston.

HANNAH'S LOST
MONUMENT

Barre is a small town located in the middle of Massachusetts that many have never heard of. A typical New England town with a small population of about fifteen hundred, it has a common that is surrounded by white-painted buildings, which include a Congregational church and its historical society. Its North Park has an old-fashioned bandstand and is the home to many war memorials, including a Civil War monument. Founded in 1774, the town is not as old as Haverhill, but it does have something that was once ours.

Hannah Duston is a local hero. She was born in 1657 and was married to Thomas Duston twenty years later, in 1677. The couple lived on the west side of the settlement in an area located beyond the Sawmill River. Over the years, they bore twelve children; eight of them were still living when disaster struck the family. On March 14, 1697, an Indian war party came into the settlement to wreak havoc and take prisoners.

Thomas was busy doing his morning chores when he spotted Indians sneaking toward his home. He grabbed his gun, mounted his horse and raced to his house as he shouted a warning. His children began to run toward a garrison house located about a mile away, while he entered his cottage to save his wife and their newborn infant.

The Indians were closing in fast, and Hannah told her husband to take care of their children as they raced toward the garrison house. They were all very young, and Thomas was agonizing over which one to save. He aimed his rifle on the nearest Indian as his children ran. In the end, they all escaped.

Back at the house, the savages told Hannah to get dressed. She had recently given birth to a daughter, Martha, and had a midwife helping her out. Mrs. Mary Neff, a widow, grabbed the child and tried to escape, but she and the child were taken captive. The Indians went through Hannah's house, taking anything that they wanted, and then they set fire to the building.

Hannah was dragged outside her home and lost one of her shoes in the scuffle. It was nearing the end of winter, and the weather could always be a problem at this time of year. The attack was swift, and the war party had killed twenty-seven and captured thirteen of the settlement's inhabitants. Anticipating pursuit, the savages set out immediately for Canada.

The new baby presented a problem to the war party. The Indians felt that the baby held Mrs. Neff back, and its crying gave the war party's position away. An Indian grabbed the child from Mrs. Neff and, before Hannah's eyes, crushed its skull against an "apple tree." The Indians moved out quickly to meet with their wives and children, who were hidden in the woods.

Some of the captives became problems as they proceeded on their way. Indians killed them and then scalped them. Hannah figured that she had walked about a dozen miles that first day. This was a remarkable feat for her considering her physical condition. Mrs. Neff no doubt helped her. Passing through an area now known as Methuen, the Indians found two oxen and immediately cut out their tongues. They cooked them and left the oxen to die in agony.

Over the next few days, the group traveled about one hundred miles. This kind of puzzles me because when they stopped along the Merrimack River, they were only about fifty miles north of the settlement. Wearing only one shoe, Hannah managed to keep up with the war party over rough terrain, some of it still covered with snow. Poorly clad, the captives suffered in the cold as they headed north along the river.

Hannah became the property of an Indian named Bampico. He took her and Mrs. Neff away from the main party, which seemed to be traveling slower than he would like. His small group consisted of twelve Indians, along with Hannah, Mrs. Neff and a fourteen-year-old boy who had been captured almost two years earlier. The Indians included two men, three women and seven children. The slower war party stopped to camp out on the east side of the Merrimack River, several miles south of Bampico's group.

Bampico led his party north to a small island, where the Contoocook River enters the Merrimack River. He had lived for a few years with a Reverend Rowlandson of Lancaster and had learned to pray in what he called the English way. He enjoyed the prayers, but he felt better when he prayed in French. Hannah asked what was going to happen to his captives, and she was told that she would be stripped and made to "run the gauntlet" once they arrived in Canada. This did not appeal to her, and she was still upset about the killing of her baby. She didn't know how her family had fared during the attack on the settlement, but she vowed to return home.

Right: The first statue to Hannah Duston was erected in Haverhill in 1861. It became a Civil War monument for fifty-nine soldiers from Barre, Massachusetts.

Below: Hannah Duston killed and scalped the Indians who captured her in 1697. She stole a canoe and returned home with a boy and her midwife.

During the night of March 30, 1697, the captives began their work. Using hatchets, they killed ten members of the war party, including two men, two women and six children. Hannah took their scalps and wrecked their canoes before leaving the island in darkness. They only traveled at night and hid during daylight hours until they reached Bradley's Brook, located in Haverhill.

In 1855, Hannah's descendants formed a group to build a monument in her name. The *Haverhill Gazette*, dated June 7, 1861, records the erection of the first monument to Hannah in town. It was an Italian marble obelisk placed on the spot where her home had been located. The association didn't agree with the spelling of her name or the location of her home. Nothing was paid on the marble shaft during the Civil War, and the installer retrieved the monument when the war ended. Over the next few years it was forgotten.

The town of Barre, Massachusetts, wanted to put up a monument in honor of the fifty-nine men who died in the Civil War. With limited funds, it agreed to take the Italian marble shaft. Duston information appearing on the obelisk was removed, and new inscriptions about the deceased were displayed. An eagle was set on top of the shaft. The town of Barre argued about the monument's placement until, surreptitiously, the obelisk was erected in North Park in 1866. It is now the pride of the town.

This marble shaft once honored Hannah Duston and was originally the first monument in the United States raised in honor of a woman. Today, Haverhill has a bronzed figure of Hannah Duston on its common, where she stands defiantly with her hatchet.

A Frontier Settlement

Hannah Duston lays claim to our past, but there is really so much history involving our community. Early settlers began to occupy our land in 1640. We seem to think that the times were untroubled, but our ancestors were encroaching on land that wasn't theirs. They weren't alone, as the French had settled north of us in an area known as New France.

Groups of people began to occupy what were known as settlements, large land areas in terms of acreage, but having small settlements. We laughed at how easily the land was purchased for our use and joked about how little it cost. Indian tribes lived in the area and really didn't understand what a few shillings meant in a purchase. They were still allowed to hunt, fish and live on the land, so selling it meant nothing to them.

However, we were actually involved in what our mother countries were calling a period of "colonization." Nobody knew what was here in North America, but there seemed to be things that could be profitable in the long run. In the beginning, it was the furs that the Indians had and the fish in our local ocean that were valuable. It wasn't long before Haverhill took its place as a "frontier settlement," and this meant inheriting all of the adversities that went with this designation.

In 1689, English colonies existed along the Atlantic Coast, while French settlements lay north of them along the St. Lawrence River and into the Great Lakes. The French had outposts in the south and along the Mississippi River Valley, while England claimed all the territory inland from its own colonies. In reality, various Indian tribes controlled this land until 1750.

At first, the English and French struggled for control of the fur trade. Later, they fought for the land between the Appalachian Mountains and the Mississippi River. They also fought for fishing rights off the coast of Newfoundland. Like many altercations, religion became a problem because the French were primarily Catholic and the British were Protestant. Out of this mess came what we know as the French and Indian Wars.

Hannah Duston is a Haverhill native. A statue stands on the town common to remember her bravery as an Indian captive in 1697.

King William's War began in 1689 and grew out of a European struggle called the League of Auburg. In the New World, Indians allied to the English raided French settlements near Montreal. The French struck back by attacking New York and New England. During March 1697, Indians raided Haverhill and carried off Hannah Duston. They learned something about the valor of pioneer women when Hannah returned on her own with a grisly tale. The Treaty of Ryswick ended this war in 1697, and both countries gave back the lands lost on both sides.

Like its predecessor, in 1702, Queen Anne's War grew out of another European conflict known as the Spanish Succession. This war was against Spain and included New England, South Carolina and Florida. It also included the French to the north when they and their Indian allies raided English frontier settlements in New England. This included Deerfield, Massachusetts, which was destroyed on October 8, 1704.

In 1708, Queen Anne's War came to Haverhill. Early in the year, a grand council was held in Montreal, and the French decided to mount an extensive engagement. It was to involve every tribe in Canada, the Abenakis, one hundred French Canadians and a number of volunteers that included several officers in the French army. The group was a formidable body of about four hundred men, with the French under the command of Dechaillons and the infamous Hertel de Rouville, the sacker of Deerfield. The Indians reported to a man called Laperrière.

In the hopes of moving this large group without being noticed, they divided themselves into two bodies. The French, with the Algonquian, St. François and Huron Indians, would take a route by the Saint-François River, and Laperrière, with the French Mohawks, was to pass by Lake Champlain. They were to rendezvous at a lake, where they would join forces with eastern tribes, including Norridgewok, the Penobscot and others.

These tribes were all enemies of the English, and they planned to attack Portsmouth and other frontier towns along the borders. The tribe at Norridgewok was under the control of a Jesuit named Pere Rale, who was a churchman, but also a Frenchman. He would send his "sauvages" into battle after Mass and communion, a kind of paradoxical way of thinking. Norridgewok is located west of Skowhegan, Maine.

The attack failed from its beginning, when a Huron was accidentally killed by a companion. This seemed like a bad start, so the Hurons deserted the group. The Mohawks pretended to develop smallpox, and they also deserted. When the army arrived at the lake, the eastern Indians failed to meet it. The end result was a force of around 250 men—a much smaller number than what they started with.

A final French and Indian attack was made on Haverhill in 1708. They killed Minister Rolfe and his wife and took many prisoners.

It is possible that the French officers felt ashamed to return to Canada with nothing to show for their efforts, and they knew that they had too few men to attack Portsmouth, so they decided to change their tactics. They decided to attack Haverhill, a small village of about thirty buildings. The group headed for Haverhill with plans to slaughter the town.

At dawn on August 29, 1708, the group managed to slip by the frontier garrisons and was almost in the town before it was seen. A gun sounded the alarm, and the enemy scattered throughout the village in every direction to accomplish its bloody work. The first person encountered was a Mrs. Smith, and she was shot as she raced from her home to a garrison. The foremost party attacked the house of Reverend Benjamin Rolfe, which had a garrison of three soldiers.

The attack was a surprise. Hearing screams, Rolfe threw himself against the door and called on the soldiers to help him. The soldiers were afraid and did nothing. In the end, Rolfe was killed, his wife was tomahawked and their child was smashed to death on a stone near the door. A Negro slave saved two other children by covering them with tubs and concealing herself.

Anna Whittaker, who also lived with the Rolfes, hid herself in an apple chest and escaped unharmed. However, the three soldiers died begging for their lives. Several of the inhabitants saved themselves by using trickery, while a Mr. Davis beat the side of a barn and yelled that the English were coming. About sixteen people were killed during the attack and many more were taken captive.

Houses were burned, and many of the frontier families suffered tremendous loss. It was August and many of the bodies began to decompose at a rapid rate. There really wasn't much time to construct coffins so an open pit was dug to bury the dead. These were the wars that Haverhill experienced for sixty-eight years. In a book entitled *Pioneers of New France*, written by James P. Baxter in 1912, he sums up the loss as those "whose blood was the cement which holds our social structure together, and whose memory we can never sufficiently revere."

Bridging Time

Haverhill, Massachusetts, began as a settlement in 1640, when a dozen men and their families pulled their boats ashore on the northern bank of the Merrimack River, near a stream located adjacent to the present-day Linwood Cemetery. The Great River, as the native inhabitants knew it, became the main link between Pentucket and the rest of the world.

Travel was possible on the land located along the southern side of the Merrimack River, but it had to be terminated upon arriving at the edge of the deep, flowing waters. Boats had to be made available to allow any desired crossings. Seven years after their arrival, the new settlers petitioned the General Court for a bridge across the river and a road to connect them overland with Andover, a village located to the south.

In May 1647, the General Court appointed a committee to "view ye river, and to make returne to ye Courte of ye necessity and charge of a bridge." The petition was denied, and the plantation was directed to provide ferry service for those desiring to cross the river. Almost 150 years would pass before the original request was granted. By then, the settlement had become a village with a population large enough to warrant a bridge. The first bridge was built in 1794.

The Haverhill Bridge

The first bridge in the village was constructed between what we now call Haverhill and Bradford, where Main Street and South Main Street cross the Merrimack River. Local history books describe the structure as consisting of three arches, each 180 feet long, resting on three rock piers. An indication that the populace was a bit skeptical about the strength of the design was that some extraordinary measures were taken to convince them of its merit.

A one-tenth-scale model of the arch was constructed, with its largest member being no greater in size than one-half-inch square. Citizens were asked to stand on it to test its strength, and it supported more than twelve hundred pounds. Perhaps the demonstration wasn't totally effective as, on opening day, a ninety-nine-year-old woman was sent to walk its length, unescorted. The Haverhill Bridge was completely rebuilt three times from 1794 to the present day.

THE MERRIMACK BRIDGE

In 1794, a group of businessmen organized the Merrimack Bridge Society for the purpose of installing a second bridge in the village. Haverhill extends a long way on the northern bank of the Merrimack River, and at least five ferries were operating to carry people, animals and goods across the river. People coming from West Newbury would benefit greatly by using a bridge at Rocks Village.

A wooden toll bridge was built across the river in 1795 and did away with the local ferry. However, a spring freshet in 1818 sent huge blocks of ice crashing against the bridge, completely destroying it. The bridge had

The Rocks Village Bridge was the second bridge in Haverhill and was erected in 1795. This is an 1893 view of the drawbridge.

existed for only twenty years, and it would be another ten years before it was replaced. A second wooden bridge was built in 1828.

THE RAILROAD BRIDGE

The railroad arrived on the Bradford side of the Merrimack River in 1837. Haverhill was growing, and it was decided to extend the tracks across the river in 1839 using a wooden bridge and a single track. The structure would also provide access for pedestrians who wished to cross. This became the village's third bridge.

The bridge would tremble whenever a train passed over it, and pedestrians on the bridge at that time would crouch behind water barrels that had been stored there for use in the event of fires caused by hot coals. The original tracks entered the village at street level, and the tracks were enclosed in what appeared to be a roofed-in structure.

It is interesting to note that what appears to be an enclosed roof running the length of the bridge was not, in reality, such a roof. A large, open slot ran its entire length and allowed the smoke from the locomotives to pass into the air above. A great deal of soot still managed to enter the passenger compartments, much to the riders' consternation.

The Railroad Bridge was rebuilt four times over the years. In 1895, a pedestrian walkway was installed for the people living in Bradford to cross over to Haverhill. In 1906, the bridge was raised above Grade Crossing and entered the city as it does now. In 1919, the iron bridge was replaced with steel. One of the trestles leading over the channel is upright, and this allowed boats to navigate the river by dropping their smokestacks.

THE GROVELAND BRIDGE

In 1870, Groveland considered its village to be a suburb of Haverhill, and many of its residents worked in the city's shoe shops. This meant that they had to either take a ferry twice a day or travel through Bradford to cross the bridge to get to and from work.

Urged on by Groveland, Haverhill agreed to become a partner in the building of its fourth bridge. Groveland was so eager to have a bridge that it assumed engineering and construction responsibilities to build it. The bridge was completed in 1872 and was the pride of the village—until it collapsed just nine years after being built.

Haverhill was a village that had no bridges until 1794 and relied on ferries to cross the Merrimack River. The Groveland Bridge collapsed in 1814.

On January 12, 1881, a span broke on the Groveland side just as a horse and wagon had begun to cross. The river was covered with ice that was so strong that it prevented anything from sinking into the river as it fell. Pedestrians placed planks atop the ice and walked across the river to their jobs in Haverhill. Reconstruction costs for the bridge repairs were divided between the county, Haverhill, Groveland and West Newbury.

Nobody really trusted the bridge, and a second metal structure was erected at this spot in 1899 at a cost of $80,000. A fire in 1913 resulted in twisted ironwork and a burned wooden deck, once again at the Groveland end. Telephone lines that ran under the bridge ignited. The wooden planks caught fire, and putting the blaze out took a great deal of time. Plans are now underway to provide a new bridge at this location.

The County Bridge

In 1903, two petitions were made to the state for another city bridge across the river. Essex County made a favorable vote, and work began in 1906. The first steel span was laid in February 1907. After its completion, pedestrians continued to walk across the Railroad Bridge, even though the two bridges were only twenty yards apart.

During 1997, the state reviewed the physical shape of all bridges located in Haverhill. Using a scale of one to one hundred, any bridge with a rating under fifty indicated major problems. The County Bridge had a rating of six! It was completely rebuilt in 2007 and is called the Comeau Bridge.

The Highway Bridge

The I-495 bridge was built as part of a government national defense plan. A network of super highways was designed and constructed across the nation to provide the military with the ability to move about the country in the most expeditious manner possible—if ever the need should arise.

The highway bridge consists of a double span located at the western side of town. This final bridge across the Merrimack River provides the quickest way to avoid the city. All of our bridges helped our city, and this one brings large trucks in and out of our town.

CATHOLICISM COMES TO HAVERHILL

Catholicism came to Haverhill during the summer of 1850, when Reverend John T. McDonnell was sent to build a church for Irish immigrants. A few years earlier, the potato crops had failed in Ireland, resulting in a great famine that drove millions from the land in search of a better life. Many came across the Atlantic Ocean to Boston, where they lived a nomadic lifestyle as they continually moved about in search of employment.

Those who came to Haverhill banded together and settled in a somewhat undeveloped section that came to be recognized as the Acre, the Irish part of town. They were devout Catholics who often traveled to Lawrence on Sundays to attend Mass. By 1850, there were enough Irish inhabitants to warrant the attention of a full-time priest. Father McDonnell, a native of Galway, came to establish a Catholic parish, the first of many that would follow.

McDonnell purchased a small tract of land at the corner of Harrison and Lancaster Streets, and in the fall of 1850, the cornerstone of the new church was laid. The original site is still occupied by the former parish grammar school, but the old brick building is now home to a few small businesses. On July 4, 1852, the original wooden church was dedicated under the patronage of Saint Gregory. Catholicism had formally arrived in the village.

The first parish still exists, but it came to be known as Saint James when a new and larger church replaced the original structure. It continued to grow until it reached its zenith in the 1930s. During that period of time, a dozen pastors had run the parish, and four of them had significantly contributed to its prominent rise in Haverhill. They were:

1850–1872   Reverend John McDonnell, founder
1878–1913   Reverend James O'Doherty, architect and builder
1913–1932   Reverend John Graham, athletics
1932–1941   Reverend Henry Lyons, spirit and spirituality

In 1852, the Irish came to Haverhill and built their church on a side street. They erected Saint James Church on Winter Street in 1884.

1850–1872

Father John T. McDonnell, a well-educated man, did more than bring the word of God to his flock. Through his efforts, a niche for Catholics was carved in an old Yankee village. He built his church on the outskirts of the village in 1850, when open fields stretched for miles in a northerly direction.

Father McDonnell taught his congregation how to save their money, purchase land and build homes in areas that bordered the church. Under his guidance, the Irish immigrants began to think in terms of permanency—to stay in one place and raise their families there. In so doing, McDonnell also helped to establish a solid workforce upon which Haverhill could rely for generations to come.

1878–1913

Saint Gregory's parish continued to grow, but always in an out-of-the-way part of the city. This all changed when Reverend James O'Doherty became the fourth pastor in 1878. He was only thirty-five years old at the time, but he was a man who could make things happen. During his thirty-five years as pastor, he moved the parish church from its side-street location to a high-profile site on Winter Street, where it took its place alongside other major churches in the city.

The new church was a red brick building with a spire that rose 215 feet into the sky. It had a two-bell belfry and a clock that rang out the time in

The wooden Saint Gregory's Grammar School burned down in 1901. A red-brick school was built in eight months and stands on Harrison Street today.

unison with city hall. His flock was so pleased with this accomplishment that it renamed the parish Saint James, in honor of O'Doherty and his patron saint.

O'Doherty immediately set about converting the old wooden church into a grammar school for the children of his parish. In 1887, he staffed it with teaching nuns from the Order of the Sisters of Saint Joseph, and it became known as Saint Gregory's Grammar School. He continued to buy land and build.

In April 1901, the grammar school burned to the ground. By September of the same year, he replaced it with a new brick building that is still standing at the corner of Harrison and Lancaster Streets. At the same time, he completed an eight-room high school on land across the street from his new church and added a second section in 1905.

1913–1932

Father O'Doherty died in 1913 and was buried in the section reserved for priests in Saint James Cemetery, located on Primrose Street. He was replaced by Reverend John Graham, who had previously served as a curate and teacher at the grammar school on Harrison Street. Father Graham had crawled into the burning building to take out samples of explosives he had used in teaching chemistry. Now he turned his attention to providing a quality athletic program for his high school students, something that was very important to the growth of the parish as well.

Father Graham fielded the first high school football team in 1917 and built a new ball field on upper Primrose Street in 1921. By that time, the high school had already achieved national recognition. It took only four years for the parish to rise in prominence, and an unabashed pride was openly displayed by students and adults alike. Father Graham had succeeded in providing a secular identity that allowed the parish to assume a more important role in the community.

1932–1941

Reverend Henry Lyons became pastor following the death of Father Graham in January 1932. He appears to have been a man who enjoyed ecclesiastical pomp and pageantry. Within a few weeks of his arrival, he directed his curates to conduct a procession in honor of the Blessed Mother, Mary. It was to involve all the children in the parish. The priests did such a good job that the event became a tradition that lasted twenty-five years. It was known as the May Procession.

During the period from 1932 to 1956, children from the parish schools wound their way along the streets near Saint James Church. A high school senior girl was chosen by her peers to be the May Queen, and she was the center of attention as she walked with her court. She wore a white gown and veil and placed a floral wreath on the head of a large statue of Mary located in the upper church. It was considered to be a great honor.

Father Lyons is also credited with coining the familiar words, "Saint James! First, last and always!" The cry can still be heard whenever former students congregate. These were the zenith years for the parish as the following years brought about many negative changes.

Saint James was a community within a community. The parish had its church, a school system, teachers, a ball field, athletes, bands and a cemetery—all in the area known as the Acre. However, in 1939, a loosened brick fell from the church's steeple to the street below. A seemingly insignificant event, it marked the first real step backward in the history of the parish. The tall spire was deemed unsafe and was removed, followed by the belfry about twenty years later.

During the next thirty years, the bands no longer marched, the ball field was closed and the athletic programs were abandoned. The nuns moved to a new convent and, in the end, they and the schools in which they taught disappeared. Like footprints in the sand, the peak years lasted only a very short while.

LIFE IN THE
MERRIMACK VALLEY

We live in an area known as the Merrimack Valley, a spot where a large river finishes its run to the sea. When Haverhill was founded in 1640, our ancestors established their first settlement alongside the Winding River, where a small stream tumbled rapidly downhill from a nearby lake. This water was used to turn the waterwheels of several mills, one after the other, next to a road that is now known as Mill Street.

Water was put to work wherever it was found. It was harnessed at the falls in Little River, in Andover along the Shawsheen River, in Methuen on the Spigot River and way up the Merrimack River, in Lowell. People used it to grind flour and corn, to drive saws and eventually to make textiles. As the Industrial Revolution developed, water provided the means to create mills that required immigrants from around the world to work in them. .

America wasn't settled overnight—it took time. Along the various waterways located throughout New England, many towns were built. Eventually, large factories were constructed, and towns such as Lowell made use of the falls in the Merrimack River to develop a series of canals that carried water to turbines located onshore.

Land along these rivers was used primarily for farming and could be purchased at a reasonable price. This was also the time for men with great minds to take advantage of circumstances. These men had visions of the future, and their thoughts, when put into action, provided undying wealth for their families. Even with great ideas, such as the proper use of steam, many still saw their futures relying on the use of water power.

There was a second waterfall on the Merrimack River located east of Lowell, between the towns of Andover and Methuen. During the early 1800s, a man had visions of doing something with it, even though it existed between two towns. Daniel Saunders, a mill owner in Andover, purchased water rights to the falls and approached other men about building a city at the site.

Knowing the power a waterfall could produce, a number of men agreed to the plan. The group approached the state for a charter on the Deer Jump Falls, and on March 20, 1845, it was granted to the Essex Company "for the purpose of constructing a dam across the Merrimack River...to use for manufacturing and mechanical purposes." After reviewing the falls on the following day, the group made plans to buy up farmland, build a dam and canals and issue stock.

Without making their plans known, the men surreptitiously bought land on both sides of the river near the falls. Saunders eventually purchased 3.5 square miles in Methuen and 3.33 miles in Andover, until he owned almost 7 square miles. They also hired engineers to design and build the world's longest dam now that they owned the land around the falls.

They hauled granite from New Hampshire and timber from Maine and laid the first stone on September 19, 1845. The Great Stone Dam eventually stretched 1,629 feet across the Merrimack River. At the same time, laborers built a mile-long canal that formed an island whose mills could tap water power from both sides. Plans also included mills and housing for the help that would work in them. The planned town was called Lawrence, after Abbot Lawrence, the major stockholder in the plan.

It is hard to imagine how people worked back in those days when one watches projects being undertaken today. By 1848, the city had grown from a few farmers to six thousand people. The plan was to use native workers to man the mills, but it wasn't long before there weren't enough local people to work there. Lawrence's textile industry advertised to the world that it had jobs and requested all types of nationalities to join it.

Workers came from everywhere to be part of the American dream. Lawrence soon became the "Immigrant City" for the world as its population increased dramatically. The workers lived in miserable conditions, with as many as one thousand in a city block. They worked long hours regulated by bells and alarms for as little as one dollar a day—twenty to thirty thousand of them. It was a city filled with people who didn't trust each other because of their backgrounds.

This was our Merrimack Valley, complete with cities designed for industry. It shouldn't surprise us to find that it was also the place where unionism found success and helped establish a middle class in this country. In January 1912, a strike broke out in Lawrence that became known as the "Bread and Roses" strike.

The workweek was reduced from fifty-six to fifty-four hours, but salaries were reduced as well. It had been difficult enough to live on their old wages, and now the people could only watch as the rich got richer while they never climbed out of poverty. It was terribly cold when they began their strike, and

The shoe district burned down in 1882 and was rebuilt in one year. This is a westerly looking view of Washington Street in 1890.

The Gardner Building survived the 1882 fire in this easterly looking view taken of Wingate Street from Railroad Square.

the National Guard was called in to control the town. A radical union, the Industrial Workers of the World (IWW), came to town to keep the workers organized against the owners.

Life was very bad, and children were sent to other states until the strike was over. There were bomb plots, and a couple of people were killed during the months the strike lasted. In the end, the workers won, but they never bragged about their accomplishment out of fear of being laid off. A couple of leaders associated with the IWW actually have their bones buried beneath the Kremlin Wall in Moscow.

Haverhill predates the cities existing up the Merrimack River. There were dams at both Lawrence and Lowell that caught the eye of textile manufacturers and led them to build these two towns. Our town only laid claim to a very small river and a minor dam. It was running water, and we built our industries along its shorelines.

There was no overall plan in place as we engaged in most industries performed along the Merrimack River. Our Yankee ancestors caught fish, built ships, raised crops and eventually started a small textile business along Little River. Farmers made shoes during the winter days when they couldn't work their farms. In the making of textiles, rivers were used for their power. In the manufacture of shoes, it was used mostly to carry away dyes and other unwanted goods associated with the trade.

Haverhill went about as far as it could in the textile business and found ways to concentrate in the manufacture of shoes. A lot of shoe jobs were done at home and people ultimately found jobs that could be done in a shoe shop. Orders were taken into a shop and the work was handed out to experts who were good at performing the task. Eventually, a trained workforce developed and was readily available to work in the business. While others became knowledgeable in the manufacture of textile, residents of Haverhill became adept at making shoes. Each city had its own special skill.

There is so much history surrounding us here in the Merrimack Valley, and much of it can be found in the local museums. Trips to Lowell, Lawrence and our own Buttonwoods are worthwhile local adventures.

Old King Coal

A recent walk turned into a stroll down memory lane. As I ambled about, I noticed a small black stone protruding from the soil near my feet. It was shiny and hard, having almost jewel-like properties. I recognized it immediately as a piece of anthracite coal, something that was in common use when I was young. Turning it over in my hand, I found myself returning to those days when coal was king.

Many homes were heated by coal when I was growing up during the Depression and World War II eras. Houses had coal-burning furnaces in their cellars, with storage areas known as coal bins usually capable of holding a year's supply of coal, about two tons for the average home. Some homes and tenements had no central heating systems, and these relied on large cast-iron stoves that also burned coal, but on a much smaller scale.

Coal was so vital to our way of life that it was a required subject in grammar school. Sometime around fourth grade, we were taught about the various types of coal available, how they formed, where they could be found and how they were mined. Our teacher, a Catholic nun, described the physical properties of each: anthracite, bituminous and sub-bituminous.

Coal yards were located throughout the city along the Merrimack River and beside the Boston and Maine (B&M) railroad tracks. The river was once used to transport large quantities of coal, but trains hauling long lines of coal cars eventually replaced boats and barges. Piles of coal were visible from both sides of the river, where railroad spurs led to sidings at coal companies like Campbell, Connell, Ham, Burchell and Taylor-Goodwin, to name a few.

There was always a mountain-sized pile of coal in the yard located outside the electric company's generating plant on Water Street. The Haverhill Gas Company stored large quantities of coke at their plant on Winter Street, where Haffner's gas station now stands. Coal could be seen just about everywhere you looked.

Coal was used everywhere in Haverhill, and it originally came by train and barge. This is a picture of a barge on the Merrimack River.

Most of the heavy machinery used during the 1930s and '40s was steam driven, equipped with boilers needing water and coal. There were steamrollers, steam shovels and large steam locomotives that hauled trains through our town. They were fascinating to watch as they hissed and belched, while being operated by men as black and greasy as they were. No matter how exciting they were to watch, I can't recall any of my friends wanting to work on them.

Coal men made deliveries year-round, but the bulk of them occurred during late summer and early fall. It took customers this long to accumulate sufficient funds to pay for them. Each October, a truck loaded with anthracite coal would pull up at our house on Dexter Street to make an annual delivery. It took two men to unload the truck. If the vehicle was able to back up to the cellar window, a long steel chute could be used from the truck to the coal bin. One man stood atop the load to keep it flowing down the chute, while the other stood inside the coal bin, spreading it evenly as it arrived.

Delivery was no easy task, and more often than not, the entire load had to be transferred a bushel at a time, all two tons of it. The two men used large canvas bags with looped handles to carry the coal. They spent the day covered in black dust from head to toe.

A full coal bin was a special moment for my father. On delivery day, he would return home from work and head for the cellar before doing anything else. I followed him as he went to the coal bin and picked up a few of the tiny black pieces to study them more closely. They clicked as he let them trickle from his hand back into the pile. He usually commented with a sense of satisfaction that his family would remain warm for another winter.

Families had to make the single delivery last as long as possible, and they delayed lighting a coal fire until they had to. Homes with hot-air furnaces, such as ours, could use small pieces of kindling wood to take away the early morning chill. Each house had a saw, sawhorse, axe and chopping block in the cellar for this purpose. My mother began each season using kindling wood that my father had cut during the warmer days of the year.

Once the coal fire was started in the furnace, it was treated with tender, loving care to keep it going. Several times during each day, a handle was attached to the furnace grates to shake down the burning coals and remove the dead ashes. These were shoveled into small pails called hods.

A few shovelfuls of coal were added to the furnace, while adjustments were made to the grilles in the door and to the flue on the chimney pipe. Each night the coals had to be banked to last the long hours until morning. It was up to my mother to provide these skills.

The hot ashes from the furnace were never thrown away. They were taken outside to be sifted into a metal ash can with a lid. I can still see my mother in our backyard as she picked over the pieces that remained in the sifter and threw them back into the hod to be burned again. I inherited this job when I got older.

Sometimes the ashes were spread on slippery sidewalks in much the same way sand is used today. This resulted in unwanted dust and dirt being tracked into the house each winter. Every spring, the rugs had to be taken outside to be beaten and swept clean. This was part of the spring-cleaning chores that were not easy.

During these early years of my life, I saw old people bundled up against the cold, carrying hods and heading for the railroad tracks, where they could pick up pieces of coal that fell from passing trains. They used them in their parlor and kitchen stoves.

The shops in town all burned coal. Large smokestacks rose in the air near the factories and smoke poured out of them all day. My house was supposed to be white, but it always appeared to be sooty paint. Most houses did. Hydrogen sulfide was getting into our lead paint.

Coal yards were built alongside railroads and the Merrimack River. Taylor-Goodwin was located along the railroad in Bradford. Both businesses have disappeared from Haverhill.

The story about coal goes back a long way in our country. When Europeans began to arrive in eastern Pennsylvania, they realized that there were vast amounts of coal there. The trouble was that it was anthracite and no one could figure out how to light it. In 1828, an enterprising Scot injected heated air into a furnace by means of a bellows, and this transformed the coal industry all over the world. The great irony of anthracite is that once it is lit, it is nearly impossible to put out. A sad part of coal mining is its death toll. Between 1870 and the outbreak of World War I, more than fifty thousand people died in American mines.

It is now strange to see cellars without coal bins, but their traces are still there.

The Railroad Comes to Haverhill

Haverhill was only a small village of about forty-five hundred people when the first railroad crossed the Merrimack River from Bradford in 1839. The tracks were laid along the quiet western part of town and headed north into New Hampshire. Most of the people lived around the Haverhill Bridge and the train depot in Bradford wasn't easy to get to. Residents worked on farms or on jobs located in the village.

Two toll bridges linked the village to other towns, and the railroad bridge became the third one to span the river. By 1840, a growing business was beginning to take shape as the village entered the industrial world. Haverhill was well on its way to becoming the "Queen Slipper City" as its shoes were being shipped around the world.

The first railroad bridge into the village was a "make-do" piece of construction that took two years to complete. Granite piers supported the span over the river, but it was raised to the street level using wooden beams. It was a single-track system with a roofed structure and covered sides designed to protect it from the weather. This type of roofing would allow the bridge to be well lighted and ventilated. The place where it entered the village was known as Grade Crossing.

Shoe shops already existed along Merrimack Street, and newer versions were being erected closer to the rails. It didn't take very long for Washington Street to become a shoe district, and by 1859, only twenty years after its arrival, the Boston and Maine Railroad decided that modifications were necessary to the tracks. It set aside $10,000 for repairs.

The public was very upset with the "cheaply got up institution" and thought that the covered bridge hid the beauty of the village from those arriving by train. They wanted it reconstructed to look like the bridge leading into Lawrence, a city located just upstream from Haverhill. The desired change would be very costly, and the railroad planned only to make substantial safety improvements.

The railroad added granite abutments on each shoreline and removed from the existing granite piers the timbered tops that raised the rails to street level, replacing them with granite from the Cape Ann quarries. The abutments were eight feet wide on the Haverhill side and ten feet wide on the Bradford end. While the population clambered for an open bridge design, the old bridge was taken down and construction began to replace it with a newer covered bridge.

Haverhill continued to grow over the next twenty years, and the railroad decided to build a two-track system to handle the increase in business north of Boston. In an amazing piece of construction, work began on September 16, 1880, on a simple pile bridge to permit the temporary passage of trains while the old bridge was being replaced. The pile bridge only took forty days to complete.

People wondered about the use of piles, but the installation of this temporary bridge was given to Ross & Lord, a reliable Boston firm that was engaged in building wharves and pile bridges. The firm's engineer stated that without ice hitting them, the pile bridges would last for ten years. In a New England river such as the Merrimack, the flowing ice could destroy the bridge. The installer was gambling that ice would form and that he would use it during construction. Workers pulled down the old bridge on the last day of October 1880, while hundreds of viewers watched.

The old bridge crossed the river at a slight angle, and its granite piers led the tracks to where they would enter the Grade Crossing. Workers immediately removed the piers that had supported the bridge because they didn't face the current. The railroad ordered granite from four quarries to ensure on-time delivery. Granite was added to increase the size of the abutments, and workers rebuilt granite piers to face the flowing river's waters. A new bridge was constructed using wrought iron.

The foundations for the new piers are sixty feet long and ten feet wide. They were from three to seven feet high, according to the depth of the river at extreme low tide. They were filled with a mixture of Portland cement and gravel. This mixture was not used on the old piers, but was described in 1880 as having been invented recently. However, the truth is that the Romans used it in making bridges more than two thousand years ago and the recipe for the mix was recently found. The cement hardens the longer it stays underwater.

On February 12, 1881, the new bridge was completed, and on February 14, 1881, the first train crossed over at twelve noon. The 40-day pile bridge was torn down, and the new tracks continued to run into town at street level. It only took 147 days to complete the installation. Working through cold weather and using underwater divers around the piers, the structure

The original railroad entered Haverhill from Bradford at street level. This is a view of the covered bridge arriving at Railroad Crossing.

was finished in a manner that would be unheard of today. Unlike earlier bridges, no provisions were made for a walkway across it, and residents complained. It took until 1895 for the state to order the railroad to include one on the bridge.

The city's shoe business continued to increase, and the use of rails increased with it. People from all around the city worked in the shoe shops, and many came from Bradford across the bridge. The new bridge was here when the shoe district burned to the ground in 1882, and fire equipment and men arriving from other towns unloaded at Grade Crossing.

Over the next twenty-five years, the town continued to grow, and the railroad experienced an increase in demand. Trains heading north and south through the city stopped at the Grade Crossing depot and continued to hold up traffic in the area. In 1906, it was decided to raise the depot above the street and, at the same time, provide a fourth bridge for people and vehicles living at that end of town.

The new Railroad Bridge involved the use of iron and granite. As the tracks were raised to cross the river on a modified Pratt Truss system, work

In 1905, the Boston and Maine Railroad decided to raise its entry into Haverhill above street level. It would no longer tie up street traffic.

began at Laurel Avenue to provide a road under them on the Bradford side for access to the new County Bridge. Even River Street had to be raised about four feet to make a gradual entry into the new depot site.

The final work on the Railroad Bridge took place in 1919, when the bridge was changed to steel. It crossed the channel with a raised truss to provide ample clearance for boats still using the river. Sailboats had ceased traveling this far upriver, and steamers with jointed smokestacks passed easily beneath the bridge. Coal barges continued to come this far upstream.

A little more than a hundred years ago, Haverhill had a world-class shoe industry that depended on the railroad to get the product to market. Today, the railroad has been reduced to a single-track system as our city still wonders how it lost its shoe business. My family once worked on shoes, and two generations waited in vain for the business to return. It never did, and it never will.

A City Burning

It was a cold and windy Friday night when Officer Wellington B. Webber noticed a small fire inside a shop while walking his beat on Washington Street. A small coal stove had been left burning overnight, and it was not unusual for them to start fires. No water was available to extinguish the flames because the weather was so cold, and Officer Webber ran to sound the alarm. Little did he know at the time that the city's shoe district would cease to exist before the sun rose the following morning.

The flickering flames were first discovered at 11:40 p.m., and residents on both sides of the Merrimack River were awakened by the shrill sound of the steam fire alarm followed by the ringing of the town bell. Haverhill firefighters arrived on the scene moments later to find the wooden structure completely involved and the fire spreading rapidly to adjacent buildings. The date was February 17, 1882, and it marked the greatest catastrophe in the city's long history. More than three thousand workers lost their jobs in the middle of winter, and entire families were affected by the blaze.

This was not the first fire that occurred within the shoe district, but it was the worst. On November 16, 1873, forty firms were destroyed when flames engulfed the Prescott Block on Washington Street. The block was destroyed, and damage was estimated to be $175,000. Over the previous years, Washington Street had been converted into the shoe district. Wooden homes first lined the river, and these were moved to Wingate Street. In their place, a series of brick buildings were built along the river's edge. On the north side of Washington Street, the buildings were a combination of wood and stone located next to each other. By the next day, all of these structures were gone.

It was bitterly cold, and a strong northwest wind fanned the flames as firemen began their fight to contain the blaze. As walls collapsed, they sent sparks flying into the night air, where they were borne across the street to buildings lining the south side of Washington Street. New fires started faster than they could be put out, and the situation was soon deemed to be out of

The Little River provided a small amount of relief where it entered the Merrimack River. It prevented the fire from proceeding along the ground.

control, despite the valiant efforts of the Haverhill and Bradford companies that had responded to the alarm.

Dispatches were sent by telegraph to the neighboring towns requesting aid. It was nearly 1:00 a.m. when they were received, and action was taken to send both men and equipment to Haverhill. By then it was impossible to save the buildings that were burning along both sides of Washington Street from Little River to the depot and from Wingate Street to the Merrimack River. The high winds carried sparks and burning debris across the river, where they started fires on some rooftops. Bradford Academy was in danger as smoke fell on and around its property.

Realizing that all was lost along Washington Street, battle lines were drawn with the intent of preventing the fire from spreading outside the shoe district. Lawrence was the first city to respond when their Steamer No. 5 arrived on the theater train. The large, boiler-operated pumps had to be transported on platform cars to their destination, and this was no easy task.

Newburyport received the dispatch at 1:00 p.m. and Mayor Hale was notified. He drove to the Boston and Maine depot to arrange for steamer transport, but the station agent refused to grant permission. He was afraid to assume the responsibility. A conductor was found who assisted in commandeering the 2:00 a.m. train to search for platform cars. Two were found on a siding, but they were frozen in ice to the tracks. Axes were used to free them, and the train left the depot bound for Haverhill at 3:00 a.m.

In the meantime, the powerful steamer from Lawrence was given the job of holding the line at Essex Street, and it was credited with saving the Washington Square area. Other units were positioned along Wingate Street and near the depot to contain the blaze. Interviewed in 1933, Fire Captain James F. O'Conner recalled how cold it was that night. As a young fireman, he was with a unit assigned to set up a pump at the underground reservoir on Washington Street, above the rail crossing. He stated, "It was so cold that the stream [from the hose] froze as soon as it hit the ground."

The sky turned orange as firemen labored and bystanders watched. At the height of the blaze, the fire could be seen as far away as Boston, where the *Boston Post* reported "A CITY BURNING" the next morning. A woman living in Georgetown, a town located six miles east of the fire, claimed to have read a newspaper by its light, out-of-doors, during the early morning hours.

There were casualties. A young fireman, Joseph St. Germain, was crushed to death by a collapsing chimney. He had been married only one month. Another fireman standing near him was rendered "senseless" by a brick from the chimney, but he survived. The Lawrence fire chief fell down a flight of stairs and had to be assisted from the scene. One foolish individual rushed into his burning shop to save its sign and nothing else. He was cheered by onlookers and was very fortunate to escape unscathed.

The strong wind kept driving the flames south along the Merrimack River, and the fire eventually burned itself out in about four hours, although flare-ups and flying sparks continued to be a problem for several more hours. A contingent of one hundred men with engines arrived from Lowell at 5:30 a.m., but they weren't needed. The city's weary firemen, who had been joined by several retired comrades during the height of the action, were hosing the burning rubble down.

As daylight broke, the full extent of the damage became obvious to all. Nothing remained standing along Washington Street, the heart of the shoe district. Almost three hundred businesses, most related to the shoe industry, had gone up in smoke, and with them went the hopes of at least three thousand workers who no longer had jobs. The city had been brought to its knees by what history now refers to as the Great Fire of 1882.

The buildings had pretty good insurance on them, and Haverhill's shoe business didn't use much machinery in shoe construction. The individual worker lost his tools, and this was a calamity. Insurance companies paid off their claims quickly, and some businesses were working the next day

On February 17, 1882, a fire broke out in Haverhill's shoe district and totally destroyed it. Buildings on Washington Street and Wingate Street were burned.

in vacated premises on Merrimack Street. A lot of shoe jobs were done at home. As the world continued turning, orders started arriving from all over the globe.

The greatest gift that Haverhill had was its own workforce, and the owners knew it. Upriver, Lawrence and Lowell had people who understood the making of textiles. In Haverhill, the workers knew about shoes. It was winter and they needed the work. Some owners placed workers in Lynn until they had their new shops built.

This event will always be remembered as one of the worst calamities to hit Haverhill, second only to the self-inflected damage resulting from its urban renewal fiasco during the 1960s.

THE PHOENIX RISES

The Great Fire of 1882 destroyed most of the buildings in Haverhill's shoe district. It began just before midnight on February 17 and burned out of control for more than four hours. Fanned by high winds, flames raced along both sides of Washington Street, consuming everything in their path. Daylight revealed that the entire area had been reduced to nothing more than smoldering piles of rubble. Those looking upon the scene felt certain that a once proud industry had also perished in the blaze.

Early the next morning, Saturday, owners with men and wagons began the task of clearing the area, even though some of the bricks were still warm. They set about retrieving their metal safes that were buried in the debris as police worked to prevent looting. Some of the owners were back in business that same day, moving into space that had been vacated at an earlier date. Others would join them during the following week.

Trainloads of spectators began to arrive at the depot, and the Boston and Maine Railroad did a landslide business over the next several days. There were no automobiles, and traveling in horse-drawn conveyances during the winter was not a pleasant option. Crowds gathered to watch a three-story-high brick wall rock in the wind near the train station, and a barricade was erected to keep them from getting too close. They wanted to see it crumble, as though it were a punctuation mark that indicated a finish to the catastrophe they had witnessed.

Mayor Moses How ordered all liquor stores closed the next day and went about establishing a relief committee for the benefit of families requiring assistance. More than three thousand workers were without jobs, and the twelve homes on Wingate Street were destroyed in the fire. The mayor also met with members of the town government to begin work on an ordinance prohibiting the construction of wood buildings in the burned-out area. This was approved on February 21, 1882.

Owner J.B. Swett was one of the fortunate ones whose property wasn't damaged by the fire, and he presented each leading hose man of Bradford's

Franklin Engine Company with a ten-dollar gold piece in appreciation of their saving his building, the Gardner Block. Others, not as lucky, were faced with a decision of monumental proportions.

Damage associated with the blaze was estimated at $2 million, but most of the businesses had some degree of insurance coverage. A few of the larger manufacturers lost machinery, but the operatives (workers) became the biggest losers when they lost their uninsured personal tools. The *Haverhill Daily Bulletin* reported on February 21:

> *Much less machinery is used in the manufacture of shoes in Haverhill than in some other cities, and much of the work has been done in private houses in the city and surrounding towns, the work will not be seriously interrupted.*

Had the fire occurred a month earlier, it would have been financially disastrous. However, large shipments of finished shoes had been sent out during January and February, and stock in the destroyed buildings was low. Businesses were gearing up for the spring orders that were now being received.

The owners recognized the extent of the damage wrought by the conflagration, but they also were aware that something more important than their buildings could be lost in an instant. The trained workforce was now without work. It was made up of a generation familiar with the need to go where there were jobs. They were basically itinerate by nature and would be lost forever if something didn't happen to keep them in the city.

With this thought in mind, the owners placed orders throughout the area for red building bricks the day after the fire, even though no reconstruction plans existed at the time. More than two million bricks came from Plaistow, New Hampshire, at a cost of ten to twenty cents per face, or common type. Even bricks still in the Amesbury kilns were spoken for. Orders for frames were placed with local lumberyards on the same day.

One of the first moves made by the city was when it passed an ordinance on February 21, 1882, prohibiting wood buildings more than 10 feet high and having more than 120 square feet from being built in the shoe district. Brick walls had to extend 2 feet above the roof as they felt the need for firewalls between property. Local authorities restrained pilfering, but some items were found across the river, on the Bradford side. These were retrieved.

Work on rebuilding started on Monday morning when owners had purchased all the red bricks that could be found throughout the Merrimack Valley. By Tuesday, despite falling snow, workers were still clearing out debris, and plans for new shops had already been laid out by thirteen businesses, all of which had already ordered parts from many suppliers.

Washington Street became a large canyon kept dark by the new shoe shops erected there. It came to be known as the Haverhill Shoe District.

By the end of the first week after the fire, most of the shoe shops were back in business, with most of the workers returning to their previous jobs in buildings located along Merrimack Street. Some owners sent workers to Lynn until they could rebuild their factories in the city. Architects were already hard at work designing new buildings, and the first structure was erected among the ruins on February 23, 1882. It belonged to Oliver Giddings, builder. The first actual brick was laid on March 2, 1882, less than two weeks after the disaster took place.

During the twelve months that followed the fire, construction continued in the shoe district, and shop after shop rose from the ashes on the ground. The shoe business was like the legendary phoenix, the desert bird that was consumed by flames, but rose from its ashes to live another five hundred years. Orders poured in from around the world as outsiders showed sympathy for the local industry's plight. It was marvelous how opponents came to the aid of their enemy.

Most of the buildings along Washington and Wingate Streets are of a similar design, but with distinctively different faces. They are thirty-three to thirty-eight feet wide and seventy to ninety feet long from the street to the river. The street-side brickwork has a unique character and sets each building apart from its neighbors. The former shoe district is actually an art form that displays the talent of the many bricklayers who labored to make a vision come true. The roadway access to the shops was designed for horse-drawn wagons and is still very narrow.

Looking east along Haverhill's shoe district, where most of the city's workforce labored. As business declined, the workers insisted that things would get better.

The story of Haverhill's ability to rebuild its shoe district in one year's time is well chronicled. The owners held an anniversary of the Great Fire on February 17, 1883, in the former Eagle House. Electric lights illuminated the dining room for the first time as the speakers applauded themselves on their having rebounded from tragedy. George C. How concluded his remarks with a toast: "Our city. She commenced her more glorious career which seemed her destruction."

Time eventually accomplished what the flames couldn't, and the shoe industry no longer exists in the city. All that remains are some old buildings and a place called Phoenix Row—ghosts from an era when Haverhill was the Queen Shoe City of the World.

THE OLD DOWNTOWN CLOCK

The city of Haverhill celebrated its 350th anniversary in 1990 and erected a large post clock on Merrimack Street to commemorate the event. It is a replica of a similar clock that became a downtown landmark in the days prior to urban renewal. The original clock is still around and can be seen standing in front of a local florist shop in Ward Hill.

The anniversary clock is actually the third of its kind to be installed on Merrimack Street, and only a few know anything about the original timepiece. It is now referred to as the Hussey Clock, and it was considered a marvel when it first appeared downtown in 1897.

The first post clock was the brainstorm of George F. Hussey, who was born in Rochester, New Hampshire, in 1837. He moved to Haverhill when he was seventeen years old and worked as a shoe cutter until 1887, when he opened a jewelry store. George was fifty years old at the time.

Hussey eventually relocated his store and workshop to the second floor at 94 Merrimack Street. In an attempt to bring attention to his place of business, he spent two years designing and fabricating his own curbstone clock. It stood sixteen feet high and had a forty-inch dial that was illuminated at night. It could also flash different colored lights at set intervals to attract the shoppers' attention. This magnificent "homemade" clock came to be recognized as the largest of its kind in New England.

George Hussey died in 1899 at the age of sixty-two, leaving behind a widow, Lidia, to run the business. The clock and Lidia remained at 94 Merrimack Street until a competitor set up a jewelry business across the street in 1905. William Charles Smith located his store on the second floor of the Daggett Building, which was located at 91 Merrimack Street, directly across the street from the big clock—a fact of which he was no doubt very much aware.

Lidia Hussey closed up her shop that year and seems to have taken her clock with her. Old picture postcards dating to about 1906 show a similar clock standing in front of Professor Bill's shine parlor at Railroad Square. The Hussey Clock was on its way to becoming only a memory.

An early view of Merrimack Street that shows the actual location of what was known as the Hussey Clock mounted on its south side.

The second clock was the creation of W.C. Smith, the jeweler who continued to conduct business at 91 Merrimack Street. He decided to duplicate Hussey's approach and had a clock made by the Waterbury Clock Company, of Waterbury, Connecticut, a well-known clock manufacturer. Smith placed an ad in the 1909 City Directory advising shoppers to "Look For The Big Clock" and added a small hand to it with the wording, "Up One Flight."

The Smith Clock was much more ornate than its predecessor, the Hussey Clock. It was the same size, but the forty-inch dial was enclosed in a fancy case mounted atop a fluted post with a Corinthian-type crown. Clocks were very useful, and towns arranged large ones to sound the time correctly. This clock was hand wound and was not the best reference for time on the street. It is this clock that eventually became the downtown landmark.

W.C. Smith owned the clock until 1936, when he sold it to another jeweler, Woodbury & McLead, which operated a business at 109 Merrimack Street. The year was not a good one for merchants, especially those doing business in Haverhill. The Great Depression was in full bloom, and the city's downtown section was inundated by floodwaters from the Merrimack River. The silt-laden waters rose and flowed through the Smith Clock. It never ran correctly after the flood.

Lacking the necessary funds to properly repair it, Smith left the curbstone clock not running. The public complained that it either be fixed or removed.

In response, the jeweler set the hands at twelve o'clock and left them that way. He sold the clock for the princely sum of fifty dollars, according to his grandson, George V. Smith.

Woodbury & McLead moved the clock to their store location at 109 Merrimack Street and later to 51 Merrimack Street, where it remained until the closing of the store in 1965. Many of us living today remember the old clock at this location, and it continued to be a landmark despite urban renewal and declining shopper activity along Merrimack Street. John F. Mcguire, a Bradford merchant with strong feelings about the future of the clock, offered to purchase it. He erected it in front of his store in Central Square, and it came to be known as the Bradford, or Mcguire, Clock during the twenty years that it stood there.

In its new location, it kept good time, and people passing by usually referred to it. The main road leading to the large Western Electric factory in North Andover went by it, and workers checked their watches against its time. However, its location in Central Square, Bradford, was a rather dangerous spot. It was perched near the curbstone and half of the clock protruded into the street.

The clock became the target of vandals and was actually knocked down two times by large trucks. Both accidents resulted in very costly repairs. Mcguire had sold his business and was trying to decide what to do with the clock, when a tractor-trailer brought it to the ground on August 20, 1988. Mcguire was distraught, sitting among the debris on the sidewalk in front of his store, trying to figure what to do with the clock. The cast-iron top was broken to pieces and he was wondering about the best way to repair it. He couldn't throw it away.

As luck would have it, Stephen A. Janavicus, a local florist, spotted the clock being repaired in an out-of-town shop and recognized it immediately. He had known it as a youngster and felt that it had a special meaning as an old-time city landmark. He approached John Mcguire, who was a friend, and they struck a deal between them. Steve became the fourth owner of the clock.

After it was repaired, Janavicus moved the clock to the Ward Hill area, where it now stands looking better than it did in its early days. Like a retired racing thoroughbred horse turned out to pasture, the old Smith Clock now stands in a quiet setting, far from the hustle and bustle it was once part of. It still tells the hour of the day with great accuracy, and anyone wishing to know the exact time need only to visit the florist shop, Flowers By Steve. There they can also see this timeless landmark.

At the time of the 350th anniversary, members of the Downtown Haverhill Partnership appealed to Janavicus to return the clock to them. He declined

Hussey died in 1899. A jeweler named Smith built a similar clock and mounted it across Merrimack Street when the Hussey Clock was removed.

to do so, but supplied a large brown and gold ribbon to decorate the replica at its dedication. The anniversary committee said the new timepiece would remain accurate and become a good luck charm. The clock hasn't been running right for some time.

Time no longer marches on—it seems to have found the home it was looking for.

THE BIRTH OF SAINT JAMES GRAMMAR SCHOOL

Newspapers were very different in 1901. The *Gazette* published on April 16 was filled with small articles taken from around the globe, and there didn't appear to be a banner line. The fire that destroyed Saint Gregory's Grammar School appeared as a four-inch article on page four in the paper.

There were no real details, and the entry read as follows: "Most earnest sympathy will be extended to Rev. James O'Doherty, his assistants and the parishioners of St. James in the loss sustained by them in the fire of last night." Many stories were associated with the fire that would have appeared on the front page of today's papers, but failed to be mentioned in 1901.

The loss of the school proved just how important it would be to have a structure made of brick. Father O'Doherty went to work immediately to build such a school. However, it was more important to find a home for his displaced students. Working with the Sisters, he found places to study for the 862 students. They were seated throughout the parish at temporary sites so that they could finish the current school year. This included the convent, parish property on Kenoza Avenue and other places. New facilities were promised for the fall.

It is hard to imagine the work involved in putting together the plans for a new grammar school. Today, a committee would be working on the project, and who knows how long it would take to build such a structure. In 1901, plans and materials were provided so that a sixteen-room building was ready for occupancy by September 1901.

The new grammar school was built where the first wooden church stood. Like much of the Acre, it was built on a hill and overlooked the railroad. It was made of red brick with a main entrance on Harrison Street. A second entrance was positioned midway along the building on Lancaster Street. Brickwork at this entrance made use of a Roman arch that is still very interesting to look at.

The ground floors contained a music/lunchroom in the northeast corner, first-grade rooms on the west side and latrines in the south center. The boy's

Saint Gregory's School burned down in 1901. An old wooden church, everything was destroyed but this statue of the Blessed Mother.

latrine had a fixed slate wall on the east side with a trough running near the feet. In the first two years of school, this arrangement provided some fun for growing boys.

The second floor included the main entrance to Harrison Street. The principal's office was located above the Lancaster Street entry, with a staircase leading to the lower level. Lighting on the second floor was enhanced by sunlight from a skylight on the roof. This was accomplished by providing a five-square-foot patch of glass on the third floor to allow the light to pass through. Two cloakroom areas existed across the aisle from the office for grades five to seven, which were located on the floor.

In a special area above the main entrance to the building, a statue of Our Blessed Mother surrounded by lace draperies was put on display. This was the same statue that survived the fire that destroyed Saint Gregory's school. Also, a new brick chapel connected the school and Saint Mary's Convent, located perhaps fifteen yards from it. The link also contained a passageway that allowed the nuns to come from their convent to school without worrying about the outside weather.

Although the parish was known as Saint James, its original students referred to the new school as Saint Gregory's. I attended the school beginning September 1938, and it was referred to either way. However, all of our school papers carried its name as Saint James Grammar School. It should be remembered that many of the older people living in the Acre had attended the school when it was known by its original parish name.

The grammar school was still run in an old-fashioned way when I started to attend. We played on Harrison Street before school, and a student with a large cowbell rang entry from the front steps. We departed the school from the Lancaster Street side as a student stood by a Victrola outside the principal's office and played a song that went something like, "When the monkey wrapped its tail around the flagpole."

The playground was located on Harrison Street just south of the convent. It was very dusty and its only pleasure was a butternut tree that grew against its back fence. I knew that the nuns weren't starving, as each day the odors from their kitchen drifted out onto the playground. The Depression was on and our meals never were as good as they were in the convent.

From September 1938 to June 1950, the parochial school system was my home. My life with the nuns began when I was six years old and ended with my graduation at eighteen years of age. As I look back on those early days of my life, I have to admit that I was more than a handful for my parents. Not a year went by that I didn't "visit" the convent with my father, mostly for talking in class.

Reverend James O'Doherty was a building pastor, and he finally built the last half of his high school on Williams Street. Changes have removed it.

Life in our classrooms was spent trying to communicate with each other without the teacher catching us. Students passed along notes, some with special codes in case they were intercepted, throughout the day. The price we paid for our indiscretions was usually severe. Have you ever stayed after school to write "I shall not talk in class" a thousand times across the blackboard? In fact, have you ever tried to explain to your parents what you were writing at the kitchen table over the weekend? Have you ever sat through a discussion between your homeroom teacher and your father, after a hard day's work on his part? These events almost destroyed life in our homes.

During my years in school, most fathers had special feelings toward the nuns. They were always right. Sisters used fathers to punish us, because this was their job. The nuns constantly overlooked mothers, and most mothers didn't like it. Husbands came home weary from work only to find that they had to dress up to visit the convent. This usually brought trouble to the home, something not needed by our mothers.

In my case, Ma learned to forge Dad's signature so well that she saved her house and me from some awful grief. It seemed that most of my troubles were connected with these notes. It bothered Ma to have to cover up my bad days, mostly because she wasn't asked to reprimand me. Believe me when I tell you that the nuns didn't know what they were doing. Ma could've been their greatest ally.

I had great friends while I attended Saint James, but I must confess that my school years were not my best years. The days were endless, but I shuddered when they handed me my diploma. I knew that my next step was a full-time job, somewhere in the shoe business. I prayed for another world war, but was very thankful for the timing of Korea.

An Old-Fashioned Winter

It is the lot of grown-ups to worry about such things as freezing cold weather, but it is up to children to enjoy it. When ice forms and snow falls, they look out at a whole new world in which to play, a winter wonderland of their own. As I watch my grandchildren romp and roll in the deep snow, I can't help but recall the time when I was young and the world was new to me.

I grew up during the 1930s, when the Depression was in full bloom and we never had the luxury of wondering what outfit we would wear on any given day. We only had one to choose from. We wore woolen clothing when winter came, most of it heavy. Women and girls donned long overcoats with scarves and kerchiefs to cover their heads. Like other boys my age, I wore corduroy knickers with knee socks, a red and black plaid lumber jacket and a matching hat with a visor and earlaps.

On extremely cold days, girls and boys alike wore snow pants at play and when they walked to school. Whenever snow fell, they wore buckled overshoes, mostly the Red Ball brand. Some boys were fortunate to have high-laced leather boots that reached almost to their knees, and they didn't have to wear rubbers or overshoes in bad weather. It made dressing much easier when leaving school at the end of the day.

Each year, at Christmastime, I would beg Ma for a pair of the leather boots, and I always was one of the fortunate ones who found them under the tree, a gift from Santa. We enjoyed getting new clothing as much as toys in those days, and the boots were special. They even had a small leather pocket with a flap that held a jackknife. Many young boys owned pocketknives, and nobody was concerned that we carried them every day. We whittled and played games with them, important pastimes in a young boy's life.

There were times when the weather became intolerably cold, when it sucked the heat from our homes. Mothers went about their houses placing pieces of cloth and clothing at windows and doors to keep out the cold.

Before the age of miracle fabrics, we wore mostly cotton and woolen cloth. This 1948 photo shows a boy wearing a woolen jacket and snow pants.

During the night, they went about the bedrooms placing overcoats and additional covers on their sleeping children. In spite of all their efforts, Jack Frost always managed to paint the inside of windows with thick crystalline patterns, some so thick that it was impossible to see out of them.

Upon waking in the morning, the children never complained. Instead, they dressed quickly and ran to the kitchen stove to get warm. A look outside at the milk bottles that had been delivered earlier attested to the severity of the day's weather. Milk was not homogenized in those days and the heavy cream remained separated. It would rise in a frozen column from the glass bottles, carrying the cardboard stopper with it.

Sometimes we had "open" winters, when the weather was cold and no snow fell. The ponds froze and were perfect for skating. My Uncle Ray would take my sister and me to Round Pond, place us on a sled and skate across the frozen surface with us in tow. It was always an exciting ride and we felt that nothing in the world could go as fast as us. We were disappointed whenever a man carrying a sail flew by on his skates like we were standing still.

One cold night, Dad took me up to Round Pond to watch men cut ice by lantern light. They had been cutting with a long saw for only a short time, but already they were standing by a fair-sized opening in the ice. A snowstorm had been forecast and the men worked hard to get the ice into storage before it struck.

The ice was hauled ashore in blocks to the icehouse located there. Blocks were placed on a rusted iron chain belt that carried them up to a chute in the side of the building. Inside the icehouse, the blocks were stored in layers, and the pile was covered with sawdust to protect the ice from melting in the warmer seasons.

Whenever snow fell, we grabbed our sleds and raced to the street in front of my house. There was no need to go in search of a place to slide because most of the neighborhood streets had been designated for this purpose by the city. There weren't many cars then, and the streets were usually not busy with any traffic. We spent entire days sliding down Deter Street and pulling our sleds back to the top of the hill for another run. Every so often, we had to take a break and go into our house to thaw out and dry our clothing. One lesson I learned at this point in my life was that it wasn't very wise to touch your tongue on a cold steel runner because it just might stick there.

One of the most exciting times on our street was when my young uncle came out of his yard with his Columbus and prepared to run it down the street. It was built like a large bobsled, but could hold six people. It had a set of sleds under it with running boards and a large steering wheel. It was heavy and had a large rope on it to help in pulling it back up the hill. My

The use of ice was part of my early life. Men would cut it with saws, like in this 1910 view of workers at Round Pond.

uncle's friends left him at the steering wheel while they shoved the Columbus from the top of the hill and leaped on. Everyone got out of the way when they started down Dexter Street.

During the 1930s, the city operated a free toboggan slide at Winnekenni Park. It was a wooden trestle-type structure that spanned the road at the top of the hill near the existing city barn. The slide was painted white and reminded me of the Salisbury Beach roller coaster whenever I saw it. Sometimes, when the snow covered the ground, Dad took me there and we shared the downhill runs.

We had to stand in a line until we reached a wooden ladder that went up the south side of the slide to a platform over the roadway. A man was stationed there whose job it was to place a toboggan on the ice-covered small platform and assist the passengers onto it. The toboggan faced another ice-covered wooden chute that dropped from the elevated platform to a trail on the hill below.

Once the riders were properly positioned on the toboggan, the operator pushed a long wooden lever that tipped the small, movable platform and started them down the chute. It was an exciting ride that Dad and I repeated several times before returning home. Haverhill did a lot of things for us during the winter months. The city even installed a hockey rink on Round Pond.

The slide is now gone, but the memory of it remains with me. It marks a time when I was young, with parents still in their early thirties, and life was good. I didn't worry about much during those days—that was Ma and Dad's job.

An Ill Wind Blows

Heavy rains had been falling for nearly a week and local rivers were beginning to overflow their banks. In the mountains far to the north, more rainwater was rushing to join the Merrimack River on its journey to the sea.

The Great River was already running much higher than normal and was showing signs of a possible repeat of the flood of 1936, a catastrophic event that took place two years earlier. River waters had risen to a record crest of thirty feet, six inches and had severely covered the town. It was obvious what damage the river could do, and the Army Corps of Engineers built a concrete floodwall behind the downtown stores. Memories of this inundation were still fresh in the minds of many, and all eyes were on the river as it slowly began to rise.

Weather forecasting during the 1930s was not as we know it today, and knowledge about hurricanes was minimal. There were no computer models or TV reports to keep the public accurately informed about impending weather conditions. Hurricanes didn't register on anybody in the town. They were totally unfamiliar with the calamity associated with the odd color of the sky and the rising wind.

Although a hurricane had been advancing along the Atlantic coastline, it was drawing very little media attention. Weather reports indicated that moist, tropical air was flowing northward and would produce heavy showers along its front. Nothing was mentioned about winds of any kind. Local predictions called for continuing heavy rains as the ill wind struck Haverhill on September 21, 1938.

It happened on a Wednesday, while the city was watching the river and I was attending school for the very first time. As I walked home with my friends after school, we were lashed by both wind and rain. The wind began to intensify and the sky took on a different color, a peculiar greenish hue. By the time I reached my house, trees were swaying and bending with each gust. There was a bit of excitement that came with the high winds, but I was glad to join my family in the safety of our home.

In 1938, we were hit by an unexpected hurricane with high winds and rain. The Merrimack River rose to the height of the Groveland Bridge.

Inside our little cottage, my mother was busy doing the daily chores demanded of a young woman with five children ranging in age from four months to eight years. Dad was working at a local diner and wasn't home. The winds began to slam against the sides of the house with increasing force, causing it to shudder. We would run from window to window to watch the violent twisting and bending of the big maple trees that surrounded us. Each observation was relayed to our mother, who continued to work calmly in her kitchen.

Our home was so much different from today's houses. We had electricity that was known to fail, and we carried what they called hurricane lamps in case there was a failure. Our kitchens were heated with range oil that was stored in two drums located in the cellar. The range oil was also available for use in the lamps. We used flat irons on the stovetop and heated water when we needed it. Our refrigeration was an icebox that was filled with ice during the warm days. The main heat was coal. In other words, in the event of a major failure in the city, we would run as usual.

As the afternoon wore on and the storm worsened, Mom went to the cellar and returned with several hurricane lamps. She washed the chimneys of each and filled their reservoirs with range oil. After testing each lamp, she set them around the house where they could be obtained if needed. Next, she filled several pots with fresh water and set them aside on the kitchen table. We were now ready to ride out the storm.

That night, as we knelt by the sides of our beds, we said prayers with more sincerity than usual before hopping under the covers. It was difficult to sleep because of the howling wind that buffeted our house. Ma would peek in from time to time and reassure us that everything was all right. We knew that she must have been worried about Dad and we had no way to contact him—we didn't have a telephone at the time.

The storm continued to swirl around outside our bedroom windows as we slept. It was the middle of the night when I was awakened by a loud explosion that shook the house. It sounded like it came from our backyard. I rushed to my window and raised the shade. The old maple tree in the yard next door had split in half! The partial trunk and limb had fallen across our picket fence, crushing it along with a small shed in an adjacent yard. The heavy winds blew all night long.

The storm came to be known as the Great New England Hurricane, with wind gusts measured up to 181 miles per hour. Although nobody was killed in Haverhill, several were injured. A large number of trees had been uprooted, and there was considerable damage to property. We were happy to see that the large maple tree in front of our house showed no ill effects from the high winds.

Damage was extensive throughout the four lower New England states. There were 183 people reported dead the next day, and they were still searching for more. Flood control along certain rivers had not yet been introduced, and the states were sweating out the rising rivers inland. National guardsmen were moved into twenty-three Massachusetts towns to prevent looting of storm-smashed stores.

Focus was once again on the Merrimack River, even as cleanup activity was taking place throughout the city. The large metal doors located at each end of the new seawall had been closed, but water was pouring in behind them. River waters were being held back, but sewage and drain water systems were backing up out of manholes. They couldn't empty into the river, especially at high tide.

Factories located along River Street were closed. There is no seawall there, and the water had reached a height of 19.7 feet in the Merrimack River. They expected a freshet in the river around midnight. The Haverhill harbormaster was taking readings at the Haverhill Bridge, while the Chamber of Commerce kept hourly contact with Manchester, New Hampshire, along with Lowell and Lawrence. They wanted to know what was going on in the river north of town.

CORPS OF ENGINEERS. U.S.A.
Haverhill, Mass.   Flood Control
Boston District   Force Account
Looking upstream from sta. 0 along
land side of sea wall showing
backfill.
79-1523.3   July 1, 1937

In 1936, Haverhill experienced a major flood. The Army Corps of Engineers built a 1937 seawall to keep the Merrimack River out of town.

Merchants removed stock from the lower floors of their downtown buildings as water began to seep into basement areas. There was some downtown flooding, but nothing as bad as what happened during the flood of 1936. The river showed signs of receding by Saturday of that week, and the city was soon able to return to business as usual. Damage to Haverhill was estimated to be $500,000.

Looking back on my life, I am amazed to notice that my mother was only thirty-one years old at the time of the hurricane. She went through the storm as if it had been part of her everyday life. I also started first grade that September, and the stormy weather turned out to be symbolic of the twelve years that I spent at Saint James School.

THE OLD WAYS OF LIFE

The Haverhill that I knew when I was growing up was much different from the one in which we now live. During the 1930s, it was sort of a patchwork community made up of sections occupied by diverse ethnic groups clinging to old ways of life.

Haverhill was still very much a Yankee town, even though many immigrants lived within its borders. Rather than settle randomly throughout the city, most chose to congregate in specific areas with others from the same ethnic group, finding comfort in their numbers. They built their own churches, where priests delivered sermons in their native tongues. Some went as far as establishing schools to ensure that their children were being raised Catholic, the religion practiced by the majority of these relocated Europeans.

The Irish were the first to arrive in large numbers, and they settled in the area we still recognize as the Acre. They were victims of a great famine that drove them from their country during the late 1840s. During a forty-year period, they built a church and school as Catholics in a former Protestant town. Greeks from the Mount Washington section of the city moved to Harrison Street in 1910 and coexisted with the Irish in a friendly manner. They usually ran corner stores, barbershops and cobbler shops.

The French arrived from Canada and settled around the Hill on streets that included Broadway and Hilldale Avenue. Like the Irish, they also built a new church and grammar school, where their native language was taught and spoken. Their children were encouraged to marry only those of French ancestry, and families actually shunned members who chose to do otherwise.

The Mount Washington area was a huge family melting pot for immigrants who arrived later. Immigrants from Italy, Poland and Armenia lived alongside Jews who had no country to call their own. Lithuanians moved in to an area off North Main Street known as Moonshine Alley, and colored people—we had no blacks back then—clustered together on Ashland Street.

Before urban renewal, downtown looked like this view of Merrimack Street, looking east. All of the buildings along the Merrimack River remained in place.

People of affluence lived in large houses throughout the section known as the Highlands. Most of the immigrant groups built their own churches in their neighborhoods with clerics from similar ethnic origins.

Bigotry was rampant in the town, and it was not uncommon to hear people refer to others as Wops, Frogs, Harps, Kikes and Chinks when discussing them. These were common folks, the laboring class of residents who were usually employed by WASPs in town.

It is interesting to note that the Irish had a caste system among themselves. Those living in the Acre were considered to be cut glass, or middle-class types, while those living in Bradford were thought to be lace curtain, or upper-crust types. A poorer group was looked down on by others who referred to them as shanty Irish.

Religious differences were a sore subject, and Catholic boys and girls were instructed not to join organizations such as the YMCA under pain of grievous sin. Parents attempted to discourage their children from marrying others of different faiths. Boys calling on girls for a first date were often met at the front door and asked by mothers, "Are you a Catholic?"

National barriers were difficult to overcome, and many a non-Irish lad who was entering the Acre in pursuit of some fair lass usually paid dearly for his efforts. Some were stoned; others experienced a pugilistic end to their amorous advances. The French remained the strictest in this manner and actually shunned those who married other nationalities for the rest of their lives.

There are many who are still living today that recall what I say to be true. I knew two grandmothers who were both totally French, and they paid the price for not marrying their own nationality. One grandmother lived in Little Canada, in Lowell, and she married an Italian. She moved out of town immediately after her wedding. She didn't wear a wedding gown, but rather a green traveling dress. Rather than use his American name, John, they referred to him as Giovanni. When she died young, she was not allowed to be buried in her family plot.

The other grandmother was prevented from marrying an Irishman. This presented some problems in her life and caused her to raise her daughters very carefully. She was born in a large family and many of her sisters lived to be quite old, but they never talked to each other. When two of them died, they were in different rooms at the same rest home and neither knew the other was there.

Things weren't much better during the previous generation in my family. I found that my original great-great-grandfather, who came over to America from West Yorkshire, England, at the same time as the Irish, had similar problems. When his son became interested in an Irish girl, he referred to her as "the Harp." He said her name like an Englishman, "T'Arp," without an *h*. The name was one that my great-grandmother lived with all her life. We knew her as Tarpy, a tenderized version of her name. She was a devout Catholic, and my great-grandfather was a Protestant who converted to marry her. He died of typhus at age twenty-eight, leaving her with two very young sons. Getting no English help, she had to return to her Irish family so that she could work and raise her boys.

Saint James Parish had the only Catholic high school in the city, and it was primarily an Irish school in the beginning. Catholics from all parts of the city, including Bradford, attended classes in the school, but many felt they didn't really belong because they were greatly outnumbered by Acre children. French boys and girls from the Hill attended Saint James High in larger numbers, but those from the Mount Washington area usually chose to attend Haverhill High and Trade Schools.

My Acre neighborhood was basically Irish, but there were others with different sounding names living there. There was a simple explanation for this. When an Irish girl married another nationality, the couple could move

White's Corner is a major intersection in Haverhill of its main streets. Urban renewal managed to demolish the entire town in this area.

back into the neighborhood with no problem. Some of my best friends did not have an Irish surname, but their mothers still carried Irish roots.

Time has a wonderful way of changing things, and nature prevails in spite of the many restrictions placed on youth. Young men and women followed their hearts when the time came to choose a mate, and ethnic barriers were gradually broken down. The original neighborhoods eventually became integrated as marriages between different nationalities resulted in their demise.

Most of the old ways of living have disappeared from the scene, and this includes the churches that were central to these diverse cultures. There were six Catholic churches in town when I was young, and Saint John the Baptist became the seventh long before they were consolidated. Only four remain at this time, and none of these have congregations consisting of a single nationality.

It is nice to know that my wife can continue to attend aerobic classes at the YMCA without being damned for her actions. Some changes are definitely for the good.

THE PEDDLERS

Transportation was rather limited when I was growing up during the 1930s. There were large orange buses that ran clockwise and counterclockwise along Cedar Street. They made downtown runs according to signs that were displayed, "Belt via Cedar" or "Belt via Arlington." Shoppers used them extensively when they were loaded down with bundles, otherwise they walked.

Automobiles were few, and one's ability to get around boiled down to the bus routes and their schedules. Men went off to work each day leaving their women somewhat stranded. When items were needed, young mothers put their babies in wicker strollers and set off to do their shopping. The advent of neighborhood markets was a blessing for most families. They were located nearby, and credit could be established with their owners.

My Acre neighborhood was typical of many throughout the city. We had several corner stores to choose from, a barbershop and a cobbler shop, where we always had our one pair of shoes repaired. As good as it was, not everything could be procured at the top of the street. Eventually, new methods of supplying items in demand came into being. If people couldn't go to the mountain, the mountain ended up coming to them.

All types of deliverymen showed up on our street; some on a regular basis, others upon request. Some delivered milk and eggs every day, while other men brought ice, coal and oil on demand. There was also a buyer, of sorts, the ragman. These men played important roles in everyday life.

Some came to our street to sell their wares, going from street to street and from door to door. These vendors included the Cushman Bakery truck, whose driver was always welcome to those who could afford him. He usually loaded a large metal tray with all kinds of bakery goods, from bread to cake, and carrying it by a large handle slung over his arm, he would knock on doors. The driver knew the houses that were the best probable customers, and he usually went directly to them. Whenever finances permitted, the housewife splurged and bought some type of special baked good as a treat

We used ice in our iceboxes when I was young. An iceman delivered it daily using a horse and buggy, similar to this old view.

for her family. As children, we watched as the driver loaded his tray, and we drooled at what we saw. Unlike the iceman, the Cushman driver never gave out free samples.

Each summer, when the growing season was in progress, a small, open-backed Model-T truck appeared on our street carrying fresh produce. Its rear end was covered by a roof and its side and back was loaded with fresh fruits and vegetables on display. A scale hung from the rear of the truck, and items were sold either by weight or by count. Although the corner stores carried similar items in most cases, there was always a feeling among customers that what the truck brought was fresher. He seemed to usually do a good business.

An older man, known as Charlie the Greek, lived at the top of Dexter Street, and he had a small garden and some chickens. Eggs could be purchased from him any time, and when crops began to grow in his small side yard, he loaded them into a wheelbarrow and walked through the streets selling them. He was a very hard worker and so serious that children stayed out of his way.

One day during the mid-1930s, a man appeared on our street carrying a pack with several pots and pans hanging from it. He seemed so different to me, and even at my young age, he aroused my curiosity. He went from door to door and eventually ended up at our house, where he spoke with Ma. She left him standing on the porch as she went back into the house to get something. She returned with one of her favorite cooking pots that was badly bent and had a small hole in it. The man was a tinker, an itinerant mender of household articles.

The period I speak of was during the Depression, when most families had very little and seldom discarded anything. So it was with old pots and pans. The tinker set about repairing the pot as I watched. First, he knocked out the dents with a hammer and a few other tools. When he had restored the pot's shape, he turned it upside down and sprinkled a small amount of sand in a circle around the hole, a tinker's dam. He melted some metal and poured it into the dam. When the metal cooled, he blew away the sand and smoothed the patch until it looked new. Ma gave him a few coins for his efforts and complimented him on the quality of his work. I don't recall ever seeing another tinker again.

My favorite peddler was a small Jewish man named Abraham Lassman, known to all as Mr. Lassman. He was a short man with long white hair and a long beard to match. He always dressed in black from head to toe, wearing a long coat with a broad-brimmed hat. Mr. Lassman was a true peddler, and he went from door to door carrying two of the largest black cases that you can ever imagine. What was in each case was every housewife's dream, and he was always welcome in her home.

Once invited inside, Mr. Lassman would open his cases and begin to display a variety of curtains, bureau scarves and linen goods. I watched as Ma exclaimed an "Oh" or "Ah" over each item. Most years she would pass, but there were times when she couldn't resist. I can still hear her now as she said, "I'll take three pairs of the organdy curtains." They were a fine muslin cloth that required a great deal of work to maintain, but Ma hung them with pride in our parlor.

We had men come by to sharpen our knives, axes and scissors. I vaguely recall a wagon with a man selling either Dr. John's Medicine or Dr. True's Elixir. All of these men are gone now, but they played a very important role in our lives. As strangers on our street, they also were diversions for children who looked forward to their arrival in the midst of playtime.

The horse-and-buggy age was drawing to a close, but many companies still used them during the 1930s. Early each morning, milk bottles could be heard rattling in yards as a horse-drawn milk cart was delivering them. We had a ragman that didn't like children, and he drove his wagon through the streets yelling for rags. If we attempted to hang from the back of his wagon, he would try desperately to hit us with his whip.

During the Depression, many a vendor drove through our streets using a horse and buggy. My father and his brother delivered milk in this manner.

The iceman delivered during hot weather, with the ice covered by a tarp to protect it from the sun. Houses advertised with a cardboard card in their front windows the size they wanted. They would position it a certain way for a five-, ten-, fifteen- or twenty-cent piece. The iceman would cut and carry the piece inside. We would pick broken samples from his wagon when he was in the house. Some of the icemen cut small pieces for us to eat on hot days.

Living a
Pedestrian Life

Born in 1932, I spent my early years living in a pedestrian world. The Depression was in full bloom and people had all they could do to pay their bills, let alone own an automobile. As a result, they did a lot of walking to get where they wanted to go.

There were so few cars in our neighborhood that driveways were almost unknown on house lots. In fact, traffic along our side streets was so light that the roads were our playgrounds. During the snowy months of winter, most of our streets were blocked off and used to sled on. Wooden horses were placed as barriers at each end of the street, and kerosene lanterns were hung from them to allow children to slide in the dark.

We walked to school with our friends, whether we attended parochial or public schools. It didn't matter because we all traveled in the same manner, on foot. Each noon, we had to walk home for lunch, while the nuns ate dinner in the adjacent convent. Our mothers had to have a hot meal ready for us so that we could return to school in time to continue our afternoon classes. We ate three meals a day: breakfast, dinner and supper. Women spent a great amount of time in the kitchen preparing them from scratch.

We walked to church usually two days a week. Being a Catholic, I spent Saturday afternoon going to confession, while Sundays were spent attending the children's Mass at nine o'clock. Saturday evenings were set aside as bath nights so that we would be sparkling clean for church on Sunday mornings. This doesn't seem to make much sense today, but it was a major undertaking back in the 1930s, when some houses didn't have bathtubs. Water was generally heated on the stovetop and poured into a washtub used for bathing. The water had to be bailed out after we were done with our ablutions.

We walked downtown whenever we needed to shop or wanted to just plain hang around. When we were young, Ma used a wicker stroller to get there with her young children, and her purchases shared the ride home with them. Living in the Acre, we sometimes enjoyed riding on the large orange

People either walked or took a bus to get around town. Note the bus in the background as people watched the Little River rise.

buses, whose routes ran both ways on Cedar Street, near our home. They were identified "Belt via Cedar" and "Belt via Arlington," depending on the direction they were traveling at the time. A ride on the bus was considered a treat.

Downtown had parking spots on both sides of Merrimack Street, but they were never filled. Most of the shoppers arrived there without the benefit of a car and would return home the same way. After World War II, ownership of automobiles increased until it became a problem finding a parking space. This brought about the development of shopping malls and their acres of free parking space. The use of automobiles also brought about the demise of downtown shopping areas as we knew them.

We walked to swimming holes to find relief on hot summer days. This usually meant walking to Primrose Street and the vacant land behind Saint James Cemetery that was home to our favorite spot, Pipes, a place where bathing suits were unknown. Sometimes we waded Little River to swim at Cashman's Field. Other times, we walked to Plug's Pond to take a dip at the public bathing area located there.

We walked from our homes to skating places during the winter months. During the daylight hours, we usually spent our time playing hockey in the cove located near our swimming hole in Little River. It was not the safest place to skate, even though the water in the cove was no deeper than four feet. It was the river's channel waters flowing just beyond it that posed a problem when our hockey pucks slid across the frozen surface. I don't think there is a friend of mine who didn't fall through the ice while skating there, and we all managed to boast about it.

A group of people watch the rising Merrimack River and the effect of the 1937 sea wall after the heavy rains of the 1938 hurricane.

Girls never skated on the river at our swimming hole, so we walked to Round Pond whenever it was safe to skate on. During the days, we continued to play hockey with our shoes used as goals. When darkness fell and we were older, we walked to the pond and skated with the girls—mostly beyond the lights near Lawrence Street that were turned on for public skating. On extremely cold nights, we built small wood fires at the rear of the pond and enjoyed the coed company to be found there.

We walked to the movies and, when we were older, walked to our dates' homes to pick them up. Girls and boys alike, most of our families didn't own cars. There wasn't any sense in becoming interested in someone of the opposite sex who lived in another town because transportation, or lack thereof, stymied one from the start. My classmates, both male and female, generally lived along the "avenues" in our Acre part of town, within a stone's throw of each other's homes. This was convenient from a social point of view because we skated and sledded together while growing up.

We walked to the cobbler shop, the barbershop, the library and to view parades. When we graduated from high school, we joined the adults in their long walks to and from work. We walked in sunshine and in rain. We walked when it snowed and on cold and windy days. We walked because we had no other choice but to do so.

A prevailing wind can usually be found coming from the west, and persons walking across the Merrimack River were exposed to them. There were many pedestrians, and the city installed windbreakers to provide relief for them while on the bridge. The Haverhill Bridge, now called Basiliere, had wooden panels installed along the concrete railing on the west side of the bridge. Evidence of their former existence can be noted in the small brass plugs that remain visible in the sidewalk. They were removed during installation and replaced by threaded bolts and brackets.

The former County Bridge, now named the Comeau Bridge, has just been rebuilt. In 1906, the bridge only had one sidewalk along its east side, so a wooden barrier was installed between it and the roadway to ward off the wind. One major problem with the installation was that pedestrians were not visible enough while crossing, causing some anxiety on their part.

Some walks were not pleasant and should have been avoided at all costs. These were the walks required to visit the convent on Harrison Street with one's parents because of troubles in the school. Parents were generally tired at the end of a day's work and they were not in the best frame of mind to listen to problems described by the nuns. The walk to the convent always seemed too short, while the trip home took an eternity.

Walking was a way of life when I was young, and some referred to it as traveling on *shank's mare*. Perhaps its greatest advantage was that one was always meeting new people most of the time. Getting around on foot might bother some, but I never minded it at all.

THE WAR YEARS

I was nine years old when I joined my parents in the parlor of our little home to listen to President Franklin Delano Roosevelt announce that the Japanese had attacked a U.S. naval base located in Hawaii. Our Pacific fleet had been all but destroyed and, being young, I thought that we had just lost a war. The date was December 7, 1941, and I went to bed that night feeling very uncertain about my future.

The enemy didn't show up the next morning, and I felt better as I watched older boys and men answering the call to arms. They were replaced by small red, white and blue banners that hung in the homes they had left behind. I listened to older men talking about working at the Portsmouth shipyard, a vastly different occupation than those found in our local shoe shops.

I watched as my Acre neighborhood prepared for war. The threat of an air raid loomed large, and every effort was made to black out the town. Streetlights, with their corrugated metal shades, were fitted with side shields that prevented them from being seen from above. Automobile headlights were covered with black shields that covered the upper half of the lens, giving them a drowsy-eyed appearance. The lighting of matches and smoking outdoors were banned during the hours of darkness. Homes were fitted with blackout drapes or shades. Air raid drills became common practice, and a warden in a helmet roamed the streets, knocking on doors wherever light was visible from the outside.

Grandma hung banners in her front window as two of her sons went off to war. I lived down the street from her and would visit often to find out how my uncle's were doing. As we talked, she continued to sew small "doughnuts" that were used to form the ear holes in aviators' leather helmets. She received no pay for her work. Ma rolled cotton bandages in our home. Neither received payment for their efforts. It was done voluntarily.

I was in the fourth grade when the war started. Prior to World War II, we always began each day with a prayer and the Pledge of Allegiance to our country. Boys and girls stood with their right arms extended, palm facing upward, and pointed toward the flag as they recited the pledge. Shortly after the war began, this practice was discontinued, and the right hand was placed over the heart. The change was made because the outstretched hand resembled the Nazi "Heil Hitler" salute.

Periodically, our school became involved in mock air raid drills. Sirens sounded and students scrambled to the space under their desks. We remained there until the "all clear" siren sounded. We were always aware that a war was going on.

Rationing began as the Office of Price Administration (OPA) set limits on scarce items. Families and businesses were allowed only so much oil and gasoline. Meat, butter and sugar were hard to come by and were rationed. Ration books were issued with small red or blue non-metal coins being used for coupon change. Oleomargarine replaced butter on most tables. It came as a white, lard-like substance in a clear bag with a yellow "blister" in it. The yellow blister was actually a food dye that was intended to be kneaded into the oleo, giving it a butter look. It tasted awful.

Each Saturday morning, Ma handed me a stack of ration coupons and it was my job to stand in line for our weekly supply of butter. No matter how much you wanted, or what you could give stamps for, one pound is all you could get. I went to Kennedy's down on Merrimack Street, where I joined a long line of shoppers waiting for their pound limit. After getting my block of tub butter, I buried it deep inside my coat pocket and headed for the Kennedy's store on Winter Street, where I repeated my routine. Sometimes I was allowed to splurge and buy a pound of tub peanut butter.

Butcher shops began to carry dark red horsemeat, pig's tails and cow's tongues as meat substitutes. I can still recall seeing a cartoon showing a butcher holding a tongue, while a woman remarked, "I'd never eat any thing out of an animal's mouth!" The butcher replied, "How would you like a dozen eggs, instead?" Humor exists even in hard times.

Silk stockings became scarcer than hen's teeth, and scrap drives became commonplace. Stockpiles of used metal became part of the local landscape as we watched men tear up trolley lines to add to them. Copper pennies were replaced by steel ones, and it was announced that an experimental soybean body for automobiles had been developed. There was a demand for all kinds of aluminum as well.

The Black Rocks section of Salisbury Beach was taken over by the military and was placed off limits to the general public. A day at the beach proved to be exciting as we watched anti-aircraft batteries shoot at a drone flying out over the ocean. Television was unknown, and people attended movie theaters to view battles being fought on newsreel. Motion pictures, such as the *The Sullivan Brothers*, sent women home with

During World War II, Haverhill had a large pile of scrap metal stored in Monument Square. The old trolley rails shown here were torn up for it.

purses full of wet handkerchiefs. Skirts were longer and churches were busier than before the war.

Manpower became a problem as more and more men went off to fight. Women filled some jobs, while many men took second jobs to keep them going. Dad offered to deliver oil for another policeman who was called to duty, and he was promised help over the weekends. Help couldn't be found, so I joined him on the truck for the next three years. I was in the fifth grade and eleven years old when I started out. Although I wasn't able to play with my friends, I was very happy to be with my father. We enjoyed our time together.

My two uncles were stationed on both sides of the globe. My oldest uncle was a thirty-eight-year-old draftee, and he was with Patton's group in Germany. My youngest uncle was only twenty years old, and he was on the Pacific Ocean. At the outset of the war, I set up a world map on my wall, made flags with pins and followed them throughout their careers. They both came home, and their mother removed the banners from the front window.

The war started during the Depression, when jobs were hard to find and pay was on the low side. Western Electric came to Haverhill in 1943, and changes appeared in the workers' lifestyle. Incomes rose, families had benefits and they were able to begin to pay off their debts.

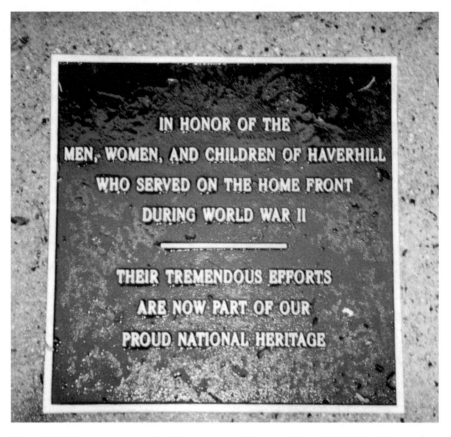

Haverhill's citizens were recognized for their contributions during World War II. I went to work with my father on an oil truck because we lacked manpower.

The war came to a conclusion in Europe, and people celebrated V-E day. A few months later, two Japanese cities disappeared in mushroom clouds, and the war was over. Bells throughout the city tolled as emotions ran at an all-time high. My uncles would be coming home and life would return to what it once used to be, or so I thought. It turned out that life, as we knew it, would never be the same. I found that much of my childhood had also disappeared during the war years.

THE WINDS OF CHANGE

More than sixty years ago, a major event took place that changed the lives of many that lived in our city. Haverhill had relied heavily on its shoe industry for generations, but it was on the decline when World War II broke out. Many shoe factories stood empty, and a once active workforce was looking for jobs to replace the ones that had been lost. The city was not alone in its plight, as other towns throughout the Merrimack Valley were experiencing similar problems.

All across the land, a male workforce went off to war leaving a manpower shortage behind. Women responded by leaving their homes to perform the jobs that were originally done only by men. The northeast region of our country was always unique because much of its female population had toiled in the mills and factories for generations. As the nation geared up for war production, cities along the Merrimack River had many vacant factories and an experienced labor pool looking for work.

In 1943, a New Jersey–based company moved some of its operations into the available manufacturing space and hired large numbers of workers who were already familiar with factory life. The Western Electric Company sent managers, supervisors, trainers and equipment to set up manufacturing facilities in both Lawrence and Haverhill. The company's arrival marked the end of the city's reliance on its shoe industry and ushered in an era of prosperity for common folk.

Western Electric came with the promise of good jobs, decent wages, good working conditions and benefits that were seldom enjoyed by the local populace. People vied for the opportunity to become employees in a Fortune 500 company known for its stability as the manufacturing branch of the Bell System, a monopolistic entity dedicated to providing the best telecommunication service in the world.

The company began its local manufacturing in buildings located on Locust and Wingate Streets. Townsfolk soon became accustomed to hearing about places such as the Grad Building, or the Hayes Building, and

Haverhill had many empty shoe shops and unemployed women when World War II broke out. Western Electric came to the city and used these facilities.

automatically knew that it involved Western Electric. Others recognized the security associated with the company in the town, and this was quite often considered during financial transactions between employees and banks when applying for loans and mortgages.

A ripple of concern appeared during the early 1950s, when the company disclosed its plans to build a plant large enough to house all of its manufacturing operations under a single roof. Residents were apprehensive when it announced its intentions to build the new plant in North Andover, just beyond the town line. Employees feared that the relocation would also mean the loss of jobs.

The new plant became known as the Merrimack Valley Works and looked more like a college campus than a factory. When facilities were moved to the new site, the employees went with them and ended up working in a state-of-the-art complex. The plant eventually grew to have two million square feet of floor space, with over twelve thousand employees in its prime.

My first actual contact with Western Electric occurred after I got out of the military in 1955. I worked for a local mover who did a lot of work for the company, and I sometimes found myself at the loading docks on Locust Street. I was surprised the first time I heard bells ring and people drop what they were doing and gather in small groups to smoke. A few minutes later, another bell rang and they went back to their tasks. The forklift operator, who wore slacks and a sport shirt on his job, impressed me.

This Pavlov's dog–like environment reinforced my intentions to never again go to work in a factory. However, I began the year 1957 working as a material handler in the new North Andover plant. My intentions were that my job would be only temporary—until I met Evie working there. We were married the following year, and I ended up spending my entire married life working there, a period of thirty-four years that ended with my retirement.

The longer I stayed with the company, the more I came to appreciate what it offered. The working conditions were always the best, and the benefits provided couldn't be found elsewhere. The company provided life insurance, medical and dental coverage, eye care, stock and savings plans that they contributed to. Vacations started at two weeks per year and expanded to six, depending on your years of service. They had a tuition reimbursement plan that, coupled with my GI bill, enabled me to obtain three degrees, including an MBA, and there were opportunities for advancement.

The company also provided a social climate for its employees that included funding for things such as basketball leagues, softball, soccer, volleyball and golf, to name a few. They held beauty contests during the early years to pick a queen who would be known as the Hello Charley Girl. Each year they held weeklong events honoring their engineers and provided recognition for perfect attendance. An on-site medical staff provided annual physicals and handled on-site injuries. In other words, nothing was ever lacking, as the company was like a third parent.

My career covered a multitude of assignments as I went from the shop to drafting and then into engineering. There were promotions along the way

Western Electric was the manufacturing branch of the Bell System. It moved into Haverhill and bought several of the old shoe shops.

and some offers that I declined, preferring to remain in the area rather than relocate to other parts of the country. I was assigned to work as a product engineer, an installation engineer and a factory engineer responsible for various facilities. I always found my work to be interesting and, in some cases, challenging.

I came from a family of six children, and all of them worked for Western Electric at some time or other. Four of our spouses worked there as well. My son and two of his cousins continue to remain with the company during its troubled times. It is obvious to all that this particular company had a great impact on my family and their lifestyles.

When I retired in 1989, I joined 450 other employees in accepting a special early offering. I really hadn't thought very much about retiring, although I was planning for the day it would happen. When I announced my intention to accept the package being offered, I was told that they hadn't expected me to take it. I was asked, "Aren't you happy here?" I replied, "What has happiness got to do with arithmetic?" I offered to return as a consultant, which I did several days later, working at my old job for another year before hanging them up for good.

Leaving my job behind, I reflected with contentment that I had done a good job while working there. More important, I felt that the company was left in good shape so that others following me could enjoy the security provided by it. This didn't happen. My company is now rapidly folding up its operations locally, and it won't be very long before it closes its doors forever. To those of us who spent a lifetime working there, it is like a death in the family—something that could never happen. Perhaps the winds of change will blow again. I sincerely hope so.

THE TRAIN WRECK

It was a cool and lonely autumn night on November 17, 1949, and most of Haverhill was pretty much shut down. A large diesel train was moving slowly through the city, pulling ninety-two cars behind its engine. It passed through the depot and started across the Winter Street overpass. The time was 12:30 a.m., the hour of night when trains leave behind only the mournful sounds that signify their passing.

The engineer and brakeman noticed a slight change in the load they were hauling. A casual look back at their rear revealed a constant string of sparks, followed by a view of cars falling off the bridge. One after the other, a total of eight cars left the tracks, with six cars falling onto the street or smashing into the Blake-Curtis warehouse, a red brick building that stood alongside the rails. In the caboose at the rear of the train, nothing strange was even noticed by the men who were assigned there.

The first two cars that fell were gondola types, filled with gravel used by the railroad to fix its rail beds. The load fell out of the open cars and covered Winter Street as the cars crashed onto the street and blocked it completely. The fireman reported that the next two cars were empty potato cars that also spun off the bridge. The next two cars carried grain and cement that fell into the Blake-Curtis building, ripping open its western side and tearing up its front. A seventh car hung suspended above the street, and the eighth car lost its front wheels, but remained upright.

Early reports about the cause of the accident said that the diesel and four cars had passed a rail switch, when it appeared to be struck awkwardly and sprung. The fifth car and succeeding cars were thrown onto a spur line. It was evident that the 4,647-ton unit wasn't going to reach Portland, Maine, that night. Known by the railroad as MP-4, the train had been put together in Mechanicsville, New York, and was made up of mostly empty cars. It was staffed with a crew made up of men from Maine, and none of the men were injured in this accident.

The Boston and Maine Railroad experienced two major train wrecks in Haverhill. In 1888, a wreck killed fourteen people on the Bradford side of the river.

On the street beneath the railroad tracks, residents of Haverhill were also lucky. A B&M cab driver had just passed beneath the bridge when he heard a noise. He turned around in time to see cars falling off the bridge onto the road. A second car was heading up Winter Street to Primrose Street, when its passengers saw railroad cars falling onto the roadway. The car was stopped in time, but their route home was blocked. Dorothy Reynolds, a passenger in her brother's car, stated that there "appeared to be a very thick fog" enveloping the area. This was no doubt due to the two gondola-type cars that had been filled with gravel.

The accident happened at perhaps the right time, if it was to happen at all. Winter Street is both a roadway and a walkway that was very busy when the Pentucket Mill was operating on Little River. Both automobiles and pedestrians coming from or going to work would have used it. Police arrived to secure the area so that nobody would get hurt near the wreckage around the bridge.

Grocery merchandise stored within the building was strewn about, and some even went spilling into the street. The owner of Blake-Curtis felt that merchandise loss would be minimal because much of the stock could still be used. This is a much different insurance attitude than one would find at an accident like this today. Many observers thought that the building would have to be razed and rebuilt.

Later reports by George Hill, of the Boston and Maine publicity office, said that it appeared to have been a broken wheel that caused the accident.

The new version of the "cause" seems to hold true as railroad ties from a point in Bradford to the wreck were deeply gouged. Unconfirmed reports indicated that pieces of the broken wheel were found way back at the Lowell Junction.

Wreckage was strewn about the area and was mixed with gravel on the street. The southbound track was in good shape, but buried under debris, and the other set of tracks were twisted and bent. They would have to be removed and replaced. Clearing the buried southbound track to allow trains to use it was the first task of the railroad crew. This would allow several trains stopped by the wreck to go through Haverhill, and this included a couple of passenger trains as well.

Cranes were brought on-site to begin the repairs. Cars had to be removed, but they weighed too much for the early crane to lift, and other cranes were brought in to help. It took until 5:00 a.m. to open the line and allow the stranded trains to drive slowly by the wreck site on a single track. The damaged northbound track was finally repaired at 10:40 a.m., and the railroad was able to operate on schedule. The railroad provided extra trains to be used from the Bradford side to Boston during the early part of the problem.

Police, firemen and highway crews roped off unsafe zones to keep the curious back. Winter Street was clogged, and clearing it became the next piece of business. It was estimated that it would take until Monday before traffic would be able to pass under the bridge. The B&M Railroad set the Blake-Curtis Company up in its warehouse offices across the street, installing phones and moving the company records to the new office location. The damaged warehouse could be lost at an estimated cost of $50,000.

Although the train wreck gave people something to talk about, another wreck occurred on January 10, 1888, when the Portland, Maine express from Boston derailed at the Bradford end of the Merrimack River Bridge. Its engine had stopped just before the bridge and slightly beyond the track's intersection with the Georgetown line. A car located midway on the train left the track, taking the remaining cars with it.

One car toppled against a water tower located by the tracks, and it fell on top of the car and the tank house, taking 100,000 gallons of water with it. Nine persons were killed outright, and five others died at the hospital within a week. One victim was a train worker who was warming up inside the tank house. The wreck also severely injured twenty-eight others. Once again, a broken wheel sent one car off the track and it drew three others with it.

Looking back at the wreck in 1949, there was little to complain about. Nobody was hurt and nobody died. I was attending Saint James High School when the accident happened, and I recall how students came in

A second wreck occurred at the Winter Street overpass in 1949. Many cars fell off the tracks onto the roadway, but nobody was hurt.

late because they had to use side streets from the Hilldale area. The wreck happened on Thursday, and Winter Street was cleared by five o'clock on Monday afternoon. Only three school days were affected. Students complained about the extra walking, but looking back, this doesn't appear to be much of an issue at all.

BOULEVARD OF DREAMS

The short stretch of divided highway that runs through the center of Haverhill was part of a plan that never really happened. It was supposed to be a section of Route 97 after it had been diverted away from the downtown area to facilitate construction of a large shopping mall along Merrimack Street. Instead, it remains as a monument to those involved in one of the greatest catastrophes ever to befall the city—urban renewal.

It all began back in 1958, when the federal government came up with their slum clearance and urban renewal plan. In an effort aimed at revitalizing old and run-down towns, the government was willing to assume 75 percent of the costs associated with any projects in this regard. Those in public office at the time decided that this was a perfect opportunity to breathe life back into Haverhill, and they came up with a grand plan that called for the clearing of everything that stood from Mill Street to Railroad Square, and from Winter and Summer Streets to the Merrimack River. The government approved the plan, and demolition began in 1966.

Phase one involved the oldest section of town, the area from Mill Street to Main Street, and was referred to as the Pentucket renewal site. Building after building gave way to the wrecking ball and bulldozer as the land was stripped of everything that stood in the way of progress.

Doubt entered the minds of those who watched the demolition of places that had been so much a part of their everyday lives. Regret replaced original feelings of optimism as they saw their library, courthouse and the Pentucket Club reduced to rubble. These were treasures that could never be replaced, and they wondered if what was taking place should be happening at all.

In the end, all that remained was a vast wasteland. Gone forever were properties that had contributed to the taxes needed by the city in its day-to-day business. By 1970, we had a new library, a colonial-style courthouse and Merrivista. In 1971, we had a strip-type shopping mall on Water Street and a ten-story apartment building near the Haverhill Bridge. Many of

A drastic demolition of Haverhill began when the federal government decided to implement its slum clearance and urban renewal plan.

the new buildings incorporated red bricks in their design, but they lacked architectural cohesion. It became obvious to those who observed what was happening that no actual rebuilding plan was being followed.

Like giant locusts, the wrecking machines crossed Main Street and began phase two, the elimination of all that stood from Main Street to Washington Square. The first building to give way to the onslaught was the Odd Fellows Hall, which had previously been damaged by fire. The renewed area was to be home to an acclimatized shopping mall, with a parking garage at White's Corner. Even GAR Park was to be expanded and further beautified.

The beautiful old city hall building that was the heart of Haverhill was torn from the landscape because it was in the way. No new one was built to take its place. By that time, people began to question the wisdom behind the massive clearance of space they were witnessing. They began to think in terms of nostalgia and preservation. Government money became harder to obtain, and the project began to be bogged down. Decisions were made that altered the original plan, and changes were incorporated that kept the banks and radio station WHAV where they were. The buildings along the waterfront were also to be spared.

The planned parking deck had to be relocated because of the changes, and it became a fourteen-year problem. It stood unused from 1978 to 1986 before it was approved, and it had become an embarrassment to the city. It was obvious to most people that the city had been damaged in the name of urban renewal.

Whenever they gazed out at the vast wasteland that had been created, residents realized that what had taken place could well be called urban removal. Phase three of the grand plan never got off the ground, as an attempt to preserve and restore what had escaped the wrecker's ball got underway. In 1977, the demolition ended with the Daggett Building on Merrimack Street.

Plans for the relocation of Route 97 continued through the removal process, and in the end, Haverhill had its own super highway right in the middle of town. It ended up being confusing to those who found themselves driving along it for the first time because it looked like it should lead somewhere. It didn't, and the new roadway almost put the owner of a local gas station on Emerson Street out of business. He spent more time giving directions on how to get out of town than he did pumping gasoline.

As for many others who were born and raised in Haverhill, urban renewal resulted in the removal of a landscape that I was familiar with and which was very much a part of my life. I look at the changes that have taken place and find it hard to believe that anything else ever existed. There are times that I sit in traffic waiting for the lights to change at White's Corner and I let my mind wander back to when things were so different.

Haverhill's city hall was built in 1861. In 1899, the building was gutted by fire, and it looked like urban renewal had started early. City Hall disappeared.

At the intersection, I can still see Atherton's furniture store and Carbone's with the Boy Scout office located above it. Around the corner was Bickum's drugstore, Chris's Fish Market and the Stein. There was Coakley's Diner, Bing's Tavern and the Elite Bowling Alleys. Looking up Main Street, I can still see the Manhatten Shop and busy Kelly and Driscoll's, where many dropped a week's pay on a drink, or two, before going home to waiting families.

On the right-hand side of the street, there was the Paramount Theater, with its war news and Bradford Junior College girls, Dr. Livingston's colonial house, the Bartlett Hotel, the Essex County Courthouse and the beautiful Pentucket Club. Across the street stood our city hall, with its large clock and a plaque indicating that it stood on the site of Harrods Tavern, where George Washington had stayed during a visit to the town.

Our high school was condemned and a new one was built in the country. Amesbury used the school when their school burned down, it was used as Northeast Community College for a while and it is now our "new" city hall. The former city hall clock is presently installed on the face of the library. We seem to be going backward, these days.

Winter Street once ran along the southwest side of GAR Park and was home to Kennedy's, where I stood in line for my family's weekly ration of butter during World War II. A little farther along was the A&P, where I worked during my final years in high school. At the west end of the park, across the street from the granite horse trough, was Tuscarora's—a Mecca for Haverhill High School students, who congregated there after class. It was one of the most popular soda fountains in town.

I mention the old-time setting to keep its memory alive. The places have gone, and sometimes I feel that much more than physical property disappeared during urban renewal. Things rather close to me also were victims of the ball and the blade.

BACK STREET BLUES

The downtown area of Haverhill bears little resemblance to the one I came to know as a youngster. Urban renewal and the advent of shopping malls took care of that. Streets I once walked no longer exist, including one I found to be the most interesting side street in the city.

Fleet Street never was much as streets go. It was only two cars wide, a narrow way that was more alley than street. Driving was permitted one way from Merrimack Street up to Court Street. From there, driving was allowed both ways to Pleasant Street. Shoppers seldom gave it notice as they walked from store to store along the main street.

Towns had a nice way of naming streets when they were growing. Very little effort went into thinking about what they were describing. There was Bridge Street, Water Street, Merrimack Street, River Street, Washington Street and our little Fleet Street. It should be recalled that Haverhill once had a small boat-building business when it was starting out. I guess that every town has a Main Street, and so does our city.

Lost in the shadows of the four-story buildings lining its sidewalks, Fleet Street was home to about twenty-five to thirty small businesses. The stores were very old and were covered with endless layers of paint. It was also home to a tavern that was frequented by patrons who were serious drinkers, men who spent their entire pay there. Women tended to avoid the street, going there only when they had to.

Back in the 1800s, Merrimack Street was a residential section, with homes lining the riverbanks. As the population grew, so did the town's shopping district. It originally clustered around White's Corner, but eventually spread westerly, displacing the homes that were in its way. The first block of buildings on the north side of Merrimack Street ended at a narrow dirt road called Fleet Street. The small street, with its shops, was an adjunct to the main area running alongside the river.

The shopping section continued to stretch until it reached the shoe district at Washington Square. Merrimack Street became a shopper's paradise, while Fleet Street remained what it always was, a seemingly out-of-the-way place that was home to a few small businesses.

During the early 1900s, the shopping district underwent many changes. Small stores and shops gave way to larger department stores as various businesses came and went in accordance with the laws of supply and demand. Some survived; others didn't. The same applied to those located on Fleet Street, as well.

I was born in 1932, and around that time there were more than twenty-five businesses operating along Fleet Street. The most notable were the Fleet Street Tavern, Pope Press, Edmund Little Company, Harry Vaughn, M&M Distributing Company and the 20th Century Bakery. The daily aroma of freshly baked goods emanated from the bakery and floated on the air outside the plant. It was enough to make one's mouth water when passing by.

My earliest recollection of Fleet Street was during the late 1930s, when Dad came home with a new bicycle for my older sister. It was a blue girl's bike with the low-pressure balloon tires common at the time. He had bought it at Herbert R. Sawyer's, a small bike shop located on the street. The business still exists today, though it was removed during urban renewal. It is now on Ginty's Boulevard, where Boris Migliori moved it to keep the business intact. He once worked as an apprentice for the original H.R. Sawyer.

I seldom had money to spend, but I always enjoyed walking about downtown just to see what was for sale. Sometimes my grandmother sent me to the bakery to buy a couple of pounds of dough that she transformed into scrumptious fried dough. Other times I joined my friend, John D., on a periodic visit to Leslie's Stamp Co. store. I usually hung back and watched as he went about purchasing singles and blocks of four. It was always an education for me, even though my collection was mostly cancelled stamps.

Most of my life I was content with what I owned, but there were times I walked down Fleet Street just to look at something I always wanted. There was a small pawnshop that always displayed sets of used drafting instruments in its windows. There were tarnished nickel-plated dividers, compasses and pens in worn, velvet-lined leather cases. They cost $1.50 per set—more than I could ever afford.

Fleet Street ran parallel to Main Street, behind the old city hall. Court Street connected it to the main drag, another short way that ran along the south side of the building. The police station was located in the city hall basement, and anyone spending time in jail was said to have spent it "under the clock." This was an allusion to the large timepiece located in the city hall belfry.

Urban renewal's second phase resulted in the removal of many small side streets and the buildings on them. Fleet Street disappeared at that time.

This was the center of town. The city hall was a magnificent structure that was torn down after only a hundred years. The city held banquets in its interior and held fights and wrestling for the community to see. Walking up the existing front steps felt good and entering the upper floors of the building felt even better. When I was young, we had a mayor and aldermen, who marched in full regalia in parades. The mayor's son died during World War II.

Dad became a policeman in 1938, when all you had to do was dial "50" to reach the station. He sometimes worked the desk, and I would visit him there. I was always fascinated by the large oak console with its ticker tape and reels that recorded signals from the various call boxes located throughout the town. In this corner of the city, along Court Street, the city had its police garage, with its Black Maria paddy wagon, and the police shooting range.

The policemen always used Fleet Street as they walked two-by-two in a column to Merrimack Street, where they veered off upon reaching their assigned beats. There were evenings I went to just watch the handsome group of men, including Dad, make the shift change. To me, it was more

Court Street ran by the city hall and connected Fleet Street with Main Street. The police garage appears on the right side of this picture.

impressive than the changing of the guard at Buckingham Palace. One night they were walking down Fleet Street, when they turned the corner onto Merrimack Street and surprised a thief with his hand in a broken jewelry store window.

Around the time of urban renewal, I was a cubmaster at a local parish. One of my jobs was to alert the boys on how the police worked in the city. I contacted the police and was invited to the station. The boys learned about fingerprinting, lockups and eventually got sprayed with tear gas in the rear parking lot on Fleet Street. I paid the price for this event.

Today, any evidence of the existence of Fleet Street can only be found on old city maps. During my time, it was once located beneath our parking deck, near the commemorative clock that now holds vigil there. I never get blue thinking about the old street, but I must confess that I was sorry to see it go.

A TROUBLED BRIDGE

A hundred years ago this year, residents of Haverhill had no bridge on the western side of town. Bradford had been annexed by the city, and many of its citizens worked on the opposite side of the Merrimack River. They had a walkway on the railroad bridge that had been installed to allow them to cross, but nothing existed for vehicular traffic in 1906.

During February 1903, two petitions were made to the state for another city bridge—one from the county, the other from the city. Its cost was estimated to be $200,000, a sum that was rather high due to the cost of land taking. On January 21, 1906, Essex County signed contracts with the American Bridge Co., of New York, to erect a bridge at a cost of $73,430. At the same time, it was decided to raise the railroad bridge above the street, and work began on that project as well.

The new bridge was known as the County Bridge, and it was the fifth bridge installed in the city. To make it work, River Street was raised four feet to meet Washington Street, and a roadway was lowered to pass beneath the tracks on the Bradford side. It had lighting, and its deck was made of planks. In the beginning, it was the county that was responsible for caring for the bridge. It installed wind barriers each winter for the benefit of pedestrians and removed them each spring.

In 1946, all bridges became the responsibility of the state. Like most things old, all bridges need occasional repairs, sometimes replacements. The old lighting was removed and replaced by florescent fixtures above the roadway. In 1965, the asphalt/wood deck was removed and replaced by metal grating. It was decided to change the name to Joseph C. Comeau Bridge in 1979. To most of us who lived in Haverhill, we still called it the County Bridge.

The bridge originally carried fifty-four tons, but the safe weight limit was reduced to three tons in 1993. In 1997, the state examined the six bridges of Haverhill using a scale of one to ten, with anything reading less than fifty needing work. The County Bridge had a rating of six! The state spent

The County Bridge was constructed in 1906, along with changes in the railroad bridge. This photograph shows its completion, looking from River Street toward Bradford.

a few years installing temporary metal cables throughout the structure and eventually closed the bridge to the public. During June 2002, the ends of the bridge were barricaded, and the walkway remained open.

The estimated timetable for rebuilding the bridge was originally set at four years. Designing the bridge was in progress, with Haverhill's Historical Committee making sure that it would be an integral part of our shoe district. The bidding process began in February 2003. To those of us living in Bradford, this schedule seemed unreasonable.

The first signs of activity began during October 2003, when the sounds of an electric saw filled the air. A handful of workers, with a dumpster, had begun removing trees and brush from the Bradford shore of the river. By the end of the month, a large crane appeared and began to drive steel into the riverbed along the Bradford side. After more than two years of waiting, we began to see things happening.

Fall weather turned into a very cold winter as the crew began to build a second roadway across the river. People attempted to explain what they were looking at. Some said that the wooden road was our next bridge, but it was being installed as a platform for the heavy equipment needed for demolition and construction. Another set of supports was installed to carry services across the river. This was not going to be an easy task.

As 2004 was coming to a close, huge cranes moved on-site and the removal of the original County Bridge had begun. The bridge was made of trestles, and a two-crane arrangement was in place that lifted each section off its piers. Piece by piece it was removed, placed on the temporary bridge, bent and taken immediately from the area. The bridge no longer existed by March 2005.

As the bridge was removed from the River Street side, steel cofferdams were being installed into the river bottom. In fact, everywhere you looked, steel was being set up. Throughout the cold winter, something was being done. Being a tidal river, there were worries about sturgeons migrating and spring floods occurring. The work sometimes looked like it wasn't going anywhere, but each time you viewed it, something had taken place.

The year 2005 was spent in removing the bridge trestles and building cofferdams around the supporting granite piers. The sound of pile drivers working on steel filled the air. Barges were moved into position to assist the work on the bridge. By February, the bridge had been dismantled and removed. Working above the river, there was no reason to stop any effort because of the fish. As March began, steel surrounded several of the piers, but the river began to rise in the spring. It wasn't long before the cofferdams were buried beneath the river's waters.

Afterward, work continued on the piers, and the large granite blocks were removed to the river's bottom. One by one they were taken away until each of the cofferdams was empty inside. As a pier disappeared, forms with rods were installed inside and new concrete piers began to rise for the bridge. Throughout the year, the river was in control of the project as it continued to rise due to heavy rainfalls. The height and current were so severe that work had to be stopped periodically.

Once again, the Merrimack River rose in the spring of 2006. Work continued on the piers in spite of it, until more rain raised the river to flood level. On May 16, 2006, the river overran its shores and once again work ceased. Much of the heavy equipment had to be removed from the construction site and placed on elevated land.

Work continued on the piers, and by the middle of 2006, they were all standing in the river. Like the Route 495 overpass, the piers had finished concrete sides. However, by the end of July, they had been covered with rough surfaces that matched the railroad bridge located alongside it. The slabs had been put on using brackets and epoxy, but they look just like the piers supporting the adjacent railroad bridge.

Back in August 2003, it was announced that a year had been removed from the schedule because a temporary walkway would not be built. However, work was halted during September 2006 because of a concrete

The County Bridge connected Haverhill with Bradford and allowed vehicles to enter the west side of the town. This 1920 view shows its trestle structure.

problem involving shafts. Shafts are put in each pier and run down into the bedrock located beneath the bridge. This puts the bridge and bedrock together in case it moves during an earthquake.

New tub girders arrived on-site in November to be installed atop the finished piers. The span is now completed, with a pair of girders designed to support the roadway. Utilities that run across the river were relocated to the space between them and are no longer noticeable.

Living in Bradford, I feel like the residents who lived here a hundred years ago without a bridge. They had a walkway—we had a troubled bridge.

LOCATION, LOCATION, LOCATION

The three most important things to consider when buying a house are location, location and location. The more I think about this axiom, the more I feel that it can be applied to communities as well. I doubt that Haverhill's first settlers could see far enough into the future to realize what a great location they chose for our city.

Haverhill is located geographically central to many of the things that New England is noted for. It is only a short ride from one of the nation's greatest cosmopolitan areas, the seacoast and mountains for outdoor enthusiasts. The city is also situated near famous historical sites that are so much a part of our American heritage and easy to visit. Like an old-time home in need of repair, Haverhill can always be fixed, but its location is of the utmost importance because it can never be changed.

We live less than a thirty-minute ride from Boston and all that it has to offer. Anything found in other major metropolitan areas can be found in the hub. Boston is home to a number of great museums, prestigious colleges, theaters, several professional sports teams and many fine eating places. A walk along its famous Freedom Trail provides people with a firsthand glimpse of our country's beginnings as they stroll through the pages of history. The railroad links our town to the state's capital and eliminates the need of an automobile to visit there.

As a senior citizen, it is possible to obtain very favorable train fares that will take one from Haverhill to the North Station and avoid traffic and parking problems. The local sports teams are successful at this time, and outstanding stage plays are constantly being presented. There is no end to the things that can be enjoyed in the "Big City."

It takes even less time to drive to the coast from Haverhill. A person has a choice of traveling there on land, in an automobile, or by boat, along the Merrimack River. The river is a beautiful stretch of water that flows through the city on its way to the sea. Its natural beauty is second to none of the many more-famous rivers that I have seen in North America and Europe.

Haverhill can use the Merrimack River to go to the seashore. In the past, steamers provided transportation to Salisbury Beach for the day.

Over the years in which we used the river to haul away refuse from our mills, the water quality was questionable. However, there are now laws that make us use it wisely.

I find it fascinating whenever I stand at the ocean's edge and realize that the spot is actually the eastern boundary of the North American continent. Looking at a global map, it is the line drawn that separates the land from the sea, and we live only a few minutes from it. Gazing out across the ocean, a person has to be impressed by the vast expanse that was crossed by our ancestors when they were first settled here.

A visitor to the coast has much to choose from. Many cities and towns have been built near the ocean and each has a local history almost as old as the first settlement in 1620. Old farms, buildings, shipyards and burial grounds are there for the viewer to see and appreciate. Most of these sites have eating places that still provide meals prepared in a manner enjoyed by those living near the sea.

A large number of Haverhill's residents spend a great deal of time frequenting the sandy beaches found at the seashore. They spend countless hours in the sun while frolicking in the waves. In so doing, they gain firsthand knowledge about tides and surf. High and low tides are understood by beachgoers as they become accustomed to the cold and rough waters associated with the North Atlantic. Only neophytes allow themselves to be tossed around by the large waves that often pound the shore. Seasoned beachgoers are readily identified by the manner in which they dive into curling breakers rather than allow them to crash onto them.

There seems to be fewer places for children to live as we did many years ago—the beaches are one of them. Cottages are owned, or rented, and allow families to enjoy time with the space to run free. The sandy beaches remain relatively untouched, and miles of beautiful sand are still available to play on. Deep-sea fishing is still an adventure, and the ocean remains endless to those who know how to sail it.

An hour's ride to the north of Haverhill, a driver sees miles of forested land and the beginning of a mountainous countryside. Spectacular panoramic views stretch from horizon to horizon, and each of New England's four seasons has something different to be enjoyed. Many spend their time hiking, camping, fishing or hunting while visiting there. Others head north to challenge slopes, where they ski or snowboard during the cold winter months.

People living in Haverhill who choose to take advantage of the city's prime location become familiar with many diversified styles of living. Some of them can be enjoyed locally, as families use the hills to slide on and the lakes to fish in. They are well versed in the ways of others who live by the sea and acquire the many skills needed to enjoy living in the woods. They also become quite cosmopolitan by virtue of the time spent in Boston. They are products of the multifaceted environment in which they live, or part of what they choose to enjoy.

We take so much for granted and don't really realize just how much we have while living in Haverhill. People coming from other parts of the country gaze in awe at things that are part of our everyday life. Some smell salt air and see the ocean for the first time. Others come to visit famous historical sites or stroll the decks of "Old Ironsides." Still some journey to the mountains to see, firsthand, their splendor and to walk in the scented woods found there. They generally return home thinking how fortunate we are to live here permanently.

As residents of Haverhill, we can all enjoy what our prime location has to offer. As far as the town is concerned, it can be whatever we choose to make it. We constantly comment on the condition of its local economy and long for the good old days when we had a flourishing shoe industry. Many who once worked there are now gone. Having lived during those times, let me tell you that working in the shops shouldn't be wished upon anyone.

During its 368-year history, the city has undergone many changes. It first had a fishing industry and built ships on the banks of the Merrimack

Haverhill is located near easily reached sites. However, the city has many interesting areas of its own, such as Whittier's birthplace and Winnekenni Castle.

River. Those industries disappeared before the coming of our world-famous shoe business, and nobody even mentioned their passing when I was young. Times change and life changes with them. It is up to us to decide what we want the city to be in the future and make positive moves in that direction. We have the best of locations. It is now up to us to make the right decisions as we rebuild the "house" we live in, our own Haverhill.

About the Author

Charles W. Turner was born and raised in Haverhill. He is a retired engineer for AT&T and holds a BS and an MBA from Northeastern University. His interests include sports, bird watching, classical guitar and genealogy. He has published more than two hundred stories in the *Haverhill Gazette* since he began writing for the newspaper in 1998. He is a frequent speaker on local history for groups such as NECCO, the Kiwanis and Methuen High, and has given talks for Local Channel 33.

Visit us at
www.historypress.net